Chapter 1 August 1995

Brent Mason was involved in the drug business. So far, his purchases have been small, as far as drug dealing goes. He was anxious to get bigger, but it's hard to find a source that is reliable and has good product consistently available. In his effort to make the big time, he knew how important it was to have a good source. Mid-level dealers need to have the product ready when the street dealers need to restock their supply. If not, they'll just find someone else who can meet their needs. Not only will the mid-level dealers go out of business by not keeping enough product in stock, there's a link of the chain that would be broken. Everybody down the line would need to change their business plan. Brent wanted to look like he was a competent supplier to the people who are dealing with the public.

Brent bought small amounts of cocaine from a man he was introduced to a few weeks earlier, named Ernie. The introduction to Ernie came from a longtime acquaintance Brent nicknamed, "Skinny Johnny". Ernie was a black man and went to high school on the eastside of San Antonio which at the time was predominantly black. Brent is white and was raised on the southside of San Antonio. The southside is predominantly Hispanic, and Brent was raised in the culture and spoke Spanish fairly well.

Brent and Ernie were the same age, 33. They both played high school football and wondered if they played against each other back in the day. Brent made a few smaller buys to test the quality of the product and the effectiveness of the seller. Brent told Ernie he was ready to buy a half kilo and Ernie said he knew just the right people to see for the sale.

Brent called Ernie and asked, "Hey Ernie, are you and your boys ready for the deal tonight?" Ernie said, "Hey, my boys are always ready, 24/7. They want to do it about eight, and they want to meet you, so they'll know you next time if you want to make another buy. The only thing is, they're in China Grove, just southeast of San Antonio. Do you mind going there?"

Brent replied, "No that's fine. I don't mind the drive. I'm a Doobie Brothers fan. In like driving through China Grove one in a while. It will be great to meet them. I want to develop a good working relationship with them. The dope has been pretty good so far and the prices are too.   I'm sure we can do business.   I'll pick you up about seven."

After the phone call with Ernie, Brent called Val, a longtime friend, "Hey Val, are you busy?" Val answered, "Not yet, but me and the boys are on the way to shoot some pool. Meet us at Rudy's. Those suckers are loaded with money, it's just after payday. We're just the men to remove it from their pockets and put it in ours."

Brent answered, "Oh man, I can't shoot pool tonight, and neither can you. I need you to go with me in a little while. I'm going to buy a half kilo from the guys Ernie knows."

Val replied, "Don't do that tonight, everybody has money. You should come shoot pool. Do that deal tomorrow. It ain't going nowhere. Tell him you got held up and have to do it tomorrow night."

Brent was getting frustrated with his old friend, "I can't, I really need to do this tonight. I already have a meeting planned with the source. You don't have to go in with me, I just want you to tag along in case it doesn't go well."

Val, becoming somewhat agitated, "I told you, I'm going to shoot pool. Do it tomorrow. If Ernie's got a decent source they'll understand. Tell them something came up. Tell them you had to go by and see about your mom. Tell them there's a water leak at your house. Tell him whatever you want to, just say you can't do it tonight." Now becoming angry himself, Brent replied, "Oh, okay, I guess the world revolves around you." As Val continued talking, trying to convince Brent not to go buy dope, Brent hung up on him.

Brent picked up Ernie on the southside of San Antonio at the hotel as planned. As Ernie got in the truck he asked, "Hey Brent, you got any booze?" Brent smiled and opened the console between the seats. Ernie looked in the console and saw a small ice chest, a bottle of Crown Royal, a couple of limes and two cans of Coca-Cola. Ernie smiled and said, "You' the man Brent." Brent told Ernie, "Why don't I mix us both one? I think we're going to do good business together. I'm excited about tonight." "You are? What are you excited about?" asked Ernie.

"I'm excited to meet your guys. You said they always had the product, that's the kind of guy's I'm looking for. I've had reports from my customers. They say they love what I've been selling lately." Ernie smiled and said, "Oh man, if you love the powder, you are going to love these guys. They're easy to do business with. They're pretty laid-back. Trust me on this one." "Oh, I trust you Ernie. Hell, I feel like we are friends. We probably even played high school football against each other. We should have met sooner," said Brent.

After a 30-minute ride out of San Antonio, Brent and Ernie stopped in front of an old house in China Grove surrounded by cornfields. Ernie pointed at the house and said, "That's the place. My boys bought it from an old farmer. They don't do any farming, they just do selling. They like it out here in the middle of nowhere. They can see people coming from a long way off. There are one hundred acres of good soft dirt to bury things in."

When they parked in front of the house, Ernie opened the truck door and got out. Ernie said, "Come on man, let's go in. You're going to feel welcome here." Brent had a five shot .38 caliber revolver in the pocket of the driver's door. He looked down at the pistol then looked toward Ernie standing outside the passenger door. Ernie was watching through the door window. Brent knew he couldn't get the pistol out without Ernie seeing him. If he could get it out, Ernie would see him put it in his pocket. He thought about it briefly and decided he didn't need it. He kept telling himself things would be fine, Ernie's been pretty reliable so far. Besides, Ernie said I would be welcome here. Brent got out of the truck and walked to the house without his pistol.

As Brent and Ernie walked to the front door, a large black man opened the door as if he'd been expecting them. As they entered the door, Ernie told Brent, "Have a seat on the couch". Brent sat down and looked back toward to the man standing inside the doorway. Brent watched him close and lock the door. He was an imposing figure to be sure. He was about six foot five and weighed at least 300 pounds. Brent thought it best to be sociable and asked, "How's it going? Thanks for having me over." The man stood silently staring at Brent with no expression.

Ernie walked back into the living room followed by another very large black man. As they walked to stand in front of Brent, the first man pulled an automatic pistol out of his back pants pocket. Surprised, Brent looked toward Ernie and saw the second man was holding a pistol too. The armed men stood on both sides of Ernie. Now rattled by this show of force, Brent looked at Ernie and asked, "What the hell was going on here? I don't feel welcome at all Ernie."

With an angry look on his face Ernie said, "Yeah well, we've got some things to discuss. You know Johnny's little brother, don't you?" Brent replied, "Yeah, I know that little son of a bitch, why? What's the problem?" Ernie raised his voice, "I talked to him yesterday as I was waiting for Johnny. He said

I should never do business with you. In fact, he said I was probably already looking at jail time. He told me you was a cop. That worries me quite a bit, Brent. So, what I want you to do is stand up, turn around and put your hands in the air."

Brent did as he was told. One of the men standing next to Ernie patted Brent down. He removed an envelope from one of Brent's back pockets and his wallet from the other. He handed the wallet and the envelope to Ernie. Ernie thumbed through the wallet and took out Brent's driver's license. Ernie then looked through the envelope and said, "That's a lot of money Brent, it looks like nine thousand dollars. Sit down." After Brent was seated Ernie said, "I see your last name is Brown. I didn't know that. I guess it's a good thing for you I didn't find a police ID in there. And, I guess it's a good thing you aren't packing a pistol. Things are working out so far. Why don't you tell me why Johnny's brother would say you're a cop?" Brent tried to explain, "I have a very good reason for that Ernie." "Boy, I hope so. I like you Brent, but I sure hate to think Johnny's brother is telling the truth." said Ernie. After a brief silence and looking at all three men, Brent smiled and said, "Oh, this is all just a big misunderstanding?"

Brent exclaimed, "That little piece of shit used to work for me once in a while. I'd send him to pick up a package of product, or money. He did a good job in the beginning but then I noticed the money was getting shorter and the dope was getting lighter. I knew he was stealing. I told him he was through, and he was lucky I wasn't going to take what he stole out of his ass. Johnny heard the conversation I was having with his brother and a few days later, he called me to see if he could have the job. He's been working for me for several years now. Johnny's little brother is pissed off and decided to cause me this problem. I'm not the violent type, but that little piece of shit is going to have to pay for this. Now, I guess it's up to you to believe me or not. Do you think a cop would drive this far out in the country by himself? There's no way anyone could follow me. Isn't that why you're doing business out here?" Ernie said, "That's a good point Brent. Okay man, I hope you don't hold it against me. Like you said, we're friends, right? Ernie looked at the man standing on his left side and said, "Go get the package. I think my man wants to buy some coke."

The man came back into the room with a package Brent believed was a half kilo of cocaine. Before picking up the package, Brent looked toward the envelope of money Ernie was holding and asked, "Do you want to count it?" Ernie replied, "No, hell I trust you, Brent. Do you want to weigh it?" Brent said, "No, I trust you to Ernie. Thanks for the enjoyable evening" and picked up the package. Brent asked Ernie, "Do you want me to drive you back into town?" Ernie, now being satisfied with his sale stated, "No, I'm going to stay here. Just let me know when you want to do it again." "Oh, I'm looking forward to it." said Brent.

Brent walked out of the house through the front door and got in his truck. As he started the engine, he looked back toward the house and was glad to see no one followed him out. He drove away slowly like nothing ever happened. As he drove back toward San Antonio, Brent's hands started shaking. He pulled to the side of the road and parked. With trembling hands, he reached for his bottle of Crown, opened it and took a long drink to calm his nerves. Brent sat there quietly for a few minutes, raised the bottle with a trembling hand, and took another drink. He was raised in a good middle-class, God-fearing home. He went to church twice a week. He never even saw a dope deal until a couple of years ago. He took another drink and wondered, how did I get myself into this?

Chapter 2 Leaving the Base

January 1983, Air Force Sgt. Brent Mason was sitting at the kitchen table in a fire station on Lackland Air Force Base. He was talking to his assistant chief, Frank Lopez, about his four-year term in the Air Force coming to an end. Frank asked, "So you'll be out of the service in two weeks back in civilian life. What are you going to do about a job? Do you have a something lined up, Brent?" Brent replied, "Boy, I sure hope so. I've been processing for the San Antonio Police Department for the last month." Being surprised Frank asked, "I didn't know that Brent. How's the processing going?" Brent said, "Great so far. I passed the physical tests. The screening board was hard. They had some salty police sergeants on the board, three of them. They asked some questions and judged by the answers." Frank asked, "What kind of questions did they ask?" Brent replied, "They were pretty tough. One of them was a question about whether you would write a relative a ticket for speeding. I had to think about that one. I knew it was tricky, I mean, do you say yes and hear them say, what kind of relative are you. Or say no and hear, are you just going to let all your relatives break the law? The best thing I could come up with was, I don't know I guess it depends on which relative it was." Frank laughed and asked, "Wow, how did that go over?" Brent said, "Not great. They seemed mad about the answer. They told me, just answer the question. You're not the one creating scenarios here. What am I supposed to say, yeah, I think I would write my mom a ticket? It just didn't seem believable to me. The answer I went with was, I've never written a ticket in my life, I've never been a policeman. It seems to me tickets are written to make people drive better. If I stopped my relative, but they were just a few miles over the speed limit, I probably wouldn't write the ticket." Frank asked, "Was that the only question?" Brent continued, "No there were two others. The next one was, what if you are about to book a drunk, you have him handcuffed and were just about to put him in the patrol car. You hear glass breaking and look behind you to see a guy breaking into a car in the parking lot. The guy is about 50 yards away. What are you going to do? Are you going to book the drunk, or catch the car burglar? I told them I think I would put the drunk in the backseat of the car and catch the burglar too, which didn't go over very well. They told me, oh you're gonna leave an unprotected drunk in the car while you catch the burglar? What if the drunk had a pocket full of money and some of his buddies were standing around. They see you put them in the car, and came over to rob him? The police procedures say you can't leave a prisoner unprotected. I had to think about that one for a minute. I didn't know what the police procedures were, but it did make sense. I had to come up with something. So, I said, in that case I'm going to go ahead and book the drunk. One of the salty old sergeants asked, what are you basing your decision on. You're going to book for a drunk for a class C misdemeanor? And you're going to let a suspect get away with a felony burglary? It dawned on me, this was a question and answer screening board. You better have a reason for your answer. I came up with the best thing I could think of. I said, I'm going to stick with the drunk. The other suspect is damaging a car and stealing property. It seems to me the well-being of the human is more important than catching a person damaging property and committing a theft." Frank said, "Boy Brent, that was a good one. How do they handle that?" Brent replied, "I think it went over pretty well. They did beat me up a little over the answer. Then they just moved on to the next question. The third question was, let's say you are driving your patrol car and you passed a commercial building at midnight. You drive by a store you know very well. You know that store closes at 8 o'clock. As you drive by you see lights on in the store. You also see three people moving around inside. What are you going to do?" Brent continued, "I've done some maintenance work at businesses on my days off from the fire department. I think I'd stop and check on it. Another one of the old policemen stood up and yelled, why don't you get in there and catch those burglars! He kind of shook me up. It took me a second, but I got back to what I was thinking. I said, well, I'm not sure they're burglars. Still on his feet the sergeant yelled, what do you mean they're not burglars, there in the store after it's closed aren't, they! I said, yes sir, but I've done some work in a store after it was closed. They could be doing maintenance, or maybe cleaning. I guess I'd have to go around the building and see if it was broken into. If not, I'd try to get them to come to the door and tell me what they're doing there. Man, that really set them off. Two of them leaned back in their chairs and started shaking their heads. The one that was still standing said, somebody gave you the answers to these questions. Who gave you the answers?" Brent then said, "I was stunned by that question. I didn't even know anybody in the police department. I said, nobody gave me the answers. I don't even know a policeman. I was just giving the best answer I could think of."

Frank asked, "Did they tell you whether or not you passed the test?" Brent replied, "No, not really, but they did lighten up before I left. In fact, all three of them got grins on their faces. They stood up and shook my hand as I was going out the door. I thought I did okay. Three days after the screening board I got a letter in the mail telling me I passed."

Frank said, "Wow, that was a tough one. Are you through with the processing?" Brent replied,

"No, all I have left is the physical, but I don't see any trouble with that. I've been fighting fires four years. If that isn't enough to prove I'm healthy, I don't know what is. I take the physical tomorrow."

Frank asked, "Why do you want to be a policeman? We're going to have an opening for a civilian driver next month. I'm sure you'd get the job. All you would be doing is trading your military uniform for a civilian uniform. You could come right back and be a driver just like you have for the past two years." Brent said, "I don't know Frank, I've always wanted to be a policeman. Besides, I'm tired of spending the night in a firehouse. Twelve twenty-four hour shifts a month is a lot of time away from the family. I like the work, but I'm ready to be home a little more." Frank said, "Well I hope it works out for you. It looks like you'll be a policeman soon."

Brent asked, "You know Eddie Graybeal on the other shift, don't you?" Frank answered, "Yeah, I know him. Isn't he getting out of the service about the same time you are?" Brent replied, "Yep, he and I are processing for the police department at the same time. It looks like we'll be in the same cadet class. The timing is great. We'll get out of the service and start a new job right away."

Two days later in a fire station, Frank saw Brent and asked, "Hey, did you have your physical yesterday?" Brent replied, "Yes, I did. They checked my vision, my hearing, and they even wanted to see if I could bend over and touch my toes. Also, I haven't had an x-ray in years, but they did an x-ray on my back."

Three days after the physical, Brent was standing in front of his home waiting for the mailman.

He expected to get confirmation he would be in the next cadet class for the San Antonio Police Department. He was so excited he could hardly stand still. The excitement was building when he saw the mail truck coming down the street. The mailman stopped in front of Brent and said, "You must be expecting something important." Anxious, Brent replied, "You're right, I've been waiting for you for hours." As the mailman handed Brent his mail, Brent said, "I sure hope you got something from the city in there?" "I think I did see something from the city, have a great day", as he handed the mail to Brent.

Brent was holding a letter from the city of San Antonio. He tore it open right where he was standing. The letter read, "The city of San Antonio appreciates your interest in applying for the police department, but you are rejected due to an existing back injury." Brent stood still staring at the letter. He read it over and over for a few minutes. He couldn't believe what he was seeing. He thought, "How can this be? Back injury, what back injury? I've never had a back problem in my life." He slowly walked back into the house and sat on the couch stunned by the letter. He spent some time thinking, this must be a nightmare. As he sat quietly alone in the house, the phone rang. He got up and walked into the kitchen to answer it. Still dazed from the news he said, "Hello." The voice on the other end said, "Hey Brent, it's Eddie Graybeal. Did you get your letter today?" Brent replied, "Yes, I did" Eddie was excited and asked, "Isn't it great, I got mine too. Can you believe it? We're going to be cops!" A dejected Brent informed Eddie, "Yeah, it's hard to believe all right. But I was rejected." Eddie was stunned and asked, "Rejected, that's not funny, Brent. You're kidding me, right?" Brent replied, "No, I'm not, and to tell you the truth Eddie, I don't really feel like talking." Brent hung up the phone and sat back down on the couch. It would be hours before the kid's got home from school and his wife was home from work. Brent thought, I have to shake this off before they get here. I don't want them to see me like this.

Brent walked into the fire station the next morning, as he did, Frank walked up to him with a question, "So how's it going? You're only have a few days left here. Are you ready to become a policeman?" Brent replied, "Oh, I'm as ready as I've ever been, but they don't want me." Frank asked, "What do you mean that don't want you? What are you talking about?" Brent said, "The back x-ray showed a very small injury I didn't even know I had. I've never felt like I had a back injury. I called an orthopedic at the hospital where Terrie works. He wanted me to bring in the x-rays, so I went back to the city doctor and picked them up. He looked at the x-rays and said I have a very small fracture in one of my discs. He said the reason I didn't know is because it doesn't cause pain or affect the way a back works. He said about 5% of the population has the same injury and doesn't know it. Most of the doctors believe it happens more often to guys that have played football for several years. They think it's a result of bending and taking blows to the top of the head." Frank asked, "Does that mean you're not going to get in?" Brent replied, "Yeah, I guess I'm looking for a job." Frank told him, "Brent, you need to go talk to the chief right now. I talked to him this morning about you leaving. He said he sure hates to lose you. He's already pulled an eligibility list to fill that civilian drivers' position. You still have time to get on the list. I know he'd like to hire you." Brent said, "Well, if you don't mind Frank, I'll go over to personnel and do just that. I have a wife and kids to feed, I can't do that without a job." Brent was hired to fill the open civilian position. He was driving fire trucks again just wearing a different uniform.

Forward to July 1990, Brent was washing a fire truck in front of the station when he saw an old friend drive up in a San Antonio police patrol car. It was Eddie Graybeal. Eddie parked the patrol car and walked up to Brent. As they shook hands, Eddie asked, "Hey Brent, how are you?" Brent replied, "Oh, I'm fine Eddie. What did you do, drive up here in your fancy patrol car and your fancy uniform just to rub my nose in it?" Eddie explained, "No Brent, you're my friend. I'm not here to give you a hard time. I'm here to give you some news I thought you might be interested in." Brent asked, "What kind of news is that?" Eddie said, "Brent, they've done away with the back x-ray. The city got sued last year under one of the federal laws about not hiring the handicapped." Brent was not impressed, "That's great Eddie, I'm glad to hear it. But what does that have to do with me, I'm not handicapped." Eddie said, "It's about the definition of the law. The way it's written is, you can't deny someone employment because of either a real, or imagined handicap. There was a guy that was disqualified just like you. He filed suit against the city. The city made a deal with him. They said they would hire him and change the physical but, they told him he would have to withdraw the suit. They didn't want him to insist on a bunch of money. He took the job and the city did away with the back-x-ray requirement. Now, they only want to see if you can bend and stretch without any trouble. Brent, that means you need to try again. There's going to be another eligibility test in two weeks. You did great on the test last time. You can do it again. And for you, the physical will be a piece of cake."

Brent tested, scored high and floated through the physical fitness test. He also scored high on the screening board and the medical physical. He was hired as a police cadet and started the police academy in January 1991. After graduation, Brent worked patrol on the west side of San Antonio for three years before being promoted to detective in December 1994. His first assignment as a detective was in the homicide office.

Chapter 3 Leaving Homicide

As Brent Mason walked toward the front of the San Antonio Police Homicide Unit. He felt like he was drowning. It was his day to handle misdemeanor assaults on a walk-in basis.

Brent wondered, is there no end to the numbers of people who are assaulted in San Antonio? Are there any civil people left in the world? Or did they hit and punch each other every day? I've already handled 12 walk-ins. If I can just get through my day in the barrel, the rest of the month I'll do aggravated assaults and murders. I'm not crazy about those either, but at least I have a little more time to work those cases. Those cases are just paperwork too. Anyway, these damn walk-ins should be done by secretary. The misdemeanor assault walk-ins say, "He punched me, or he slapped me." It's just taking notes, typing it up and sending it to the DAs office. The DAs office will probably get it and rejected it. Or, send it back for further investigation. Or the girlfriend complaining about how her boyfriend pushed her will be back in love tomorrow and call here to say she no longer wants to press charges.

Brent thought back to the day he was promoted to detective. Man, I couldn't have been more excited when Sgt. Campbell talked to me after the promotion ceremony. He said he wanted me in homicide. I felt so proud. I felt smart. Now I hate it. Two years of knuckle heads killing each other. Wives in the middle of divorce coming in to file charges on their husband. All because he looked at her the wrong way while picking up little Bobby Friday night. I really need to transfer. Maybe robbery, no that couldn't be much different than here. Sex crimes is definitely out. I couldn't handle the stuff with the kids. I'd just beat the hell out of a suspect and end up in prison. I don't know what I'll do, but I know I can't take this much more.

It was 4 o'clock and quitting time is six. Brent just finished interviewing another misdemeanor assault victim. He was walking his last customer of the day to the front of the office. Rene, another homicide detective, was walking in the opposite direction.

Rene was amused by the look on Brent's face. Rene knew Brent from the old patrol days. Rene thought, that boy looks like he's hating life right about now. He never looked that way back when we were working West patrol. I think he had more fun when he was having foot chases trying to catch a crook.

As they passed in the hallway, René asked, "Cadillac?"

Brent responded, "Yep."

After interviewing the last misdemeanor assault victim, Brent looked up at the large office clock. He had to stand to see it. His work station wasn't an office, it was what they referred to as, a "cubby." An 8 x 8 space bordered by four short walls. No door, just a gap in the wall big enough for a human being to walk through. Just one more thing about homicide that bothered him. He thought, we look like a bunch of damn gophers. Every time we stand to talk or look at the clock, our heads pop up over the top of the cubby walls. It just isn't dignified. What was this, some damn architect's idea of a joke? Maybe they did it to save money on two by fours and sheet rock. Maybe they were just beating the city out of money. Or maybe, they just thought it would be funny.

As Brent stood looking at the clock, Rene's head popped up over his cubby walls. He looked back at Brent and said, "Well, how did your misdemeanor day go?"

"Well let's see, how did the day go? There was a guy who came in here and wanted to file charges on a bouncer. He said he was drunk at a club and the bouncer asked him to leave. Seems reasonable to me, but he didn't think so. He threw a mug of beer in the bouncer's face. The bouncer grabbed him by the back of the shirt and the belt. He threw him through the front door and into the parking lot."

"Did the bouncer hurt him?"

"Oh, he was a little dinged up. He had a few scratches on his four head and arms where he hit the pavement. And that's what he calls an assault.

I told him, that's not an assault. You're the one that committed an assault. I think you better get out of here before I figure out who the bouncer is and file an assault case on you."

"Is that all you got, I've had some sillier than that."

"No, I got another one. There's plenty to choose from. Don't get me wrong, I like helping the people that need help. But some of them are just trying to get back at someone else and using us to do it.

There was a lady that came in with her four-year-old son. She sat down and told me how her ex-husband assaulted her. She said she went to his house to pick up her son after a visit. The ex-husband got mad at her, slapped her and pushed her down in the front yard. I asked her if she had any injuries. She said yeah, I got some scratches on my arm and shoulder. She had a long sleeve blouse on, so I asked Mona to take her into the locker room and photograph the injuries.

While she was gone, I struck up a conversation with the little boy. I ask him if he had brothers or sisters, and if he had any pets. He told me no brothers or sisters, but they did have a cat. Just out of curiosity I asked him if he saw what happened between his mom and dad. He said, yes, I did, it was pretty bad.

I kind of hated to put him through it again, but I thought I could use it in the prosecution guide if he was a witness. So, I asked, why don't you tell me what happened.

The first thing he said was, boy did mommy hurt dad. I was thinking, hold the phone, and asked him to tell me about it. He said mommy knocked on the door and dad opened it. Then mommy came in and turned over a table in the living room. It was made of glass and had a jar on top that was full of marbles. When mommy turned the table over it broke and marbles went flying everywhere. Then she kicked dad right in the, you know where. Dad yelled and fell down on the floor and we left.

Just when the boy stopped telling me what happened, his mom walked back in. I didn't want to tell her exactly what her son said, but I did say, I don't think your story is going to hold up. I think it's best if you and your son go home. She started yelling about what her ex-husband did to her. I said, yeah well, I'm not buying it. Have a nice day."

"Well I have to admit the second story was better than the first. Now I have a question for you."

"Okay Rene, hit me!"

"You about ready for the Cadillac?"

"Yeah, I could use a beer. These people are killin' me."

They ripped their ties off simultaneously and threw them down on their desks. As Brent and Rene walked through the double doors of the building and onto Nueva Street, Brent raised both hands in the air and exclaimed, "Freedom".

René laughed and responded, "It's strange how much funnier I think it is when someone else has walk-ins. It's just not as funny when I have to do them."

"Yeah René, I almost slapped the crap out of you in the hallway at 4 o'clock."

"Oh, so you knew exactly what time it was when I mentioned Cadillac?"

"Dude, I'm aware of every hour, every minute and every second of the day when I have walk-ins."

After walking two blocks on Nueva Street, both men looked up to see purple neon lights across the top of an old rock building. The neon spelled, "Cadillac Bar."

Brent said, "After a long day when I see that neon sign, it feels like arriving at an oasis in the desert. A watering hole for the weary. You would think some of our coworkers would join us. I wonder why we go to a beer joint instead of going on a run like the others. Or maybe we should go to the gym."

"Why don't you shut the hell up, Brent. The days over, lighten up. As far as running goes, I might see you run to the Cadillac, but I don't think I'm going to see you running on the River Walk."

When they walked through the front door of the Cadillac, they shook hands with the owner, Jesse. Then their eyes scanned the room for familiar faces. They looked along the front of the bar first, then looked over the tables around the small dance floor.

They walked up to the bar and Brent said, "I wish Jesse would get a waitress or two to work at six. Then we wouldn't have to stand at the bar waiting for a beer."

While waiting for the bartender to notice them, Brent looked back at Jesse standing near the front door and said, "That Jesse is really something. I think he remembers the name of every person that has ever walked in that door. Is he from San Antonio?"

René answered, "No, he's from the other side of the border. He crossed the river near Laredo when he was just a teenager. As he traveled north, he made money working in the fields of South Texas. When he got to San Antonio, he got a job here as a dishwasher. Thirty-five years later he owns the place. He's a great American success story don't you think, Brent?"

"Yeah, he's quite a dresser too. Every time I've ever seen him, he's in a nice suit and covered in gold."

"He's a sharp dresser all right. Have you noticed his Rolex?"

"Yeah Rene, I've noticed. Something tells me he didn't get it at a high-end jewelry store. I bet he got it from a customer at closing time paying off a huge bar tab." Brent thought for a second and said, "He makes you feel kinda special, doesn't he Rene?"

Rene smiled and said, "He sure does. He treats us the same way he does millionaires coming in to spend a couple thousand buying drinks for the house. He strikes me as a guy that really appreciates his success, and his customers."

After the bartender handed Brent and René their beers, they turned and walked to one of the many open tables.

At a table across the bar room sat four middle-aged men. An assistant district attorney. A criminal defense attorney. A paralegal and an adult probation officer. As Brent and René took their seats, the assistant DA made eye contact with Rene. Rene jumped to his feet and walked toward the DA's table. Brent watched Rene and thought, Rene has some of the personality traits Jesse possesses. He's a handshaker and a back slapper. If you didn't know better when you saw Rene networking, you'd think he was a politician.

Brent thought, we've only been in the bar for five minutes and already Rene's running off to talk to someone else. Hey, that's just Rene.

Networking wasn't Brent's style. He isn't the kind of man seeking new buddies or trying to convince others to like him. If Brent likes you, he'd do anything for you. He just doesn't like that many people. Brent sat quietly and drank his beer.

As Rene reached the other table, the handshaking and backslapping began. Rene pulled up a chair and sat down without being asked. The ADA asked Rene, "Isn't your buddy going to join us?"

"No, he's not in a very good mood."

"What's the matter with him?"

"Oh, he had misdemeanor walk-ins today. It'll take him a while to shake it off."

"Maybe he'd be happier in another office, Rene."

"Yeah, he's got two years in homicide and will be eligible for a transfer. I figure he'll probably try to go to another unit."

"What do you mean, try?"

"Well, sometimes they let you leave, and sometimes they don't. Sometimes they think your too valuable to let you go. That's a bitch, isn't it. I mean, you do a good job while you're in an office and what's your reward, you can't leave."

The probation officer asked Rene, "Where did he work patrol?"

"He and I were pretty hard hitters on the Westside. We made DI off the same list. I think he misses the good old days chasing crooks and fighting once in a while. As for myself, I'd rather wear suits and not have to fight anymore. These days I choose to use my superior intellect to solve crime, rather than brute force. I find that sort of thing barbaric. Brent's kind of old school. He thinks it's fun."

The defense attorney said, "Hey, to each his own."

Rene finished chatting with the, "important people". He walked back to the table where Brent was sitting staring at the tabletop. Rene sat down said, "Hey man, snap out of it. You won't have walk-ins for another month."

Without looking up Brent said, "Oh you're back. I thought you would spend the rest of the night kissing the bigwigs asses."

"Hey, that's not kissing ass, that's networking. You know, making contacts. You're just shortsighted. People like that can help you out someday."

"I have enough site to know a kiss ass when I see one. Besides, what can they do for you, get you promoted?"

"No, but you never know. It's best to hobnob with people in high places. It can't hurt. You just never know."

Brent took another swig of his beer and set it down on the table with a thud. Then said "Well, I guess I'm just not as ambitious as you. Maybe you can get me on your security staff when you're elected mayor."

"Oh no Brent, I would never have you on my staff. You're too hard to get along with. I would need people that are more refined and tactful than you. You wouldn't be working for me 10 minutes before you pissed somebody off and I'd have to fire you."

Only hard-core regulars were in the bar at six. About a quarter of the seats in the house were taken. The place was relatively quiet, and it was easy to hear the creaking of the front door when it opened. Each time the door creaked, the regulars would look to see who was coming in. When the door creaked open again, Brent and Rene looked to see who was arriving. It was two Hispanic males about 40 years old. One was slightly taller than the other and wearing black plastic frame glasses. His hair was cut over the ear and he was well dressed.

The other just looked like an old hippie, maybe even a Vietnam era veteran. His hair was shoulder length and he sported a goatee. He wore a black, "Bad Company", concert T-shirt and jeans. The two were somewhat of an odd couple. Brent thought they were a little suspicious looking.

Brent turned to Rene and said, "Why don't you go over there and see what those two pecker woods can do for you."

Rene had a big laugh at that remark. In fact, his laugh seemed a bit inappropriate to Brent.

Brent rudely asked, "Was it that funny?"

"Oh, I'll go over there and talk to them, but there's not a damn thing they can-do for me. You're right though, they are pecker woods. They're police pecker woods. The one with the glasses is Val Martinez. The other is Harry Corona. Harry's name is really Jaramillo, but they call him Harry. They both work narcotics."

"Well they could have fooled me. Do they do undercover work?"

"Yeah, Val is probably the best undercover man in the history of the department. You know, it always seemed funny to me Val is a good UC man. He graduated high school from a pretty rough school on the west side. He wasn't one of the rough customers, he was the president of the library club."

Rene and Brent laughed, and Brent asked, "I wonder how the president of the library club ends up being the best UC man in the history of the department. It's a far leap from nerd to narc."

Rene said, "Yeah, now on the other hand, Harry has the look and the ability to be one of the best, he just doesn't have the drive. Hell, people he doesn't even know ask him if the he wants to buy dope. He has to beat them off with a stick."

"Why does he tell them no? Isn't buying dope the point of being in narcotics?"

"Yeah, but if you make a case, it has to be typed up, and Harry's lazy. Come on, I'll introduce you to them."

They walked toward the bar where Harry and Val were standing. Harry saw them coming and nudged Val. "Hey, look who's coming. If it isn't the politician."

Just as suspected, Rene offered a big handshake and said, "Hey, what are you boys up to?"

Val said, 'Hello Rene, how are you?"

"I just came over here to see you two pecker woods."

As Val and Harry frowned, Val asked, "Pecker woods?"

"Yeah, that's what my friend here, Brent said when you walked in."

Brent turned to stare at Rene trying to burn a hole in his head. From Brent's angry stare at Rene, Val and Harry knew the, "Pecker wood", comment was meant to embarrass Brent.

While smiling Val said, "I guess that does describe us to a certain extent. What do you think Harry?"

"Yeah, I guess you could say that."

Trying to recover from his embarrassment, Brent stuck out his hand to Val and said, I'm Brent Mason. I work with this asshole", tilting his head toward Rene.

Harry and Rene started a conversation then walked toward the table where Rene was schmoozing earlier.

Val asked Brent, "How long have you been in homicide?"

"Let's see, one year, eleven months and four days. But who's counting?"

"Wow, you must be enjoying it to know exactly how long you've been there."

"No, I'm looking forward to the two-year mark. I'm going to put in for a transfer as soon as I'm able."

"Where do you want to go?'

"I haven't given it much thought. Sex crimes is out, but pretty much anything else is an option."

"Have you thought about going to narcotics, Brent?"

"No, I haven't. I just know I need to get out of that damn paper pushing office. I'd like to get back to doing some hands-on police work."

Val smiled and suggested, "Maybe narcotics is right for you. We're only in the office long enough to have rollcall. Then we decide where to go eat. That seems to be the biggest decision of the day. There's three or four days a month we sit around the office and type up cases. But other than that, were running around most of the time."

Brent looked over at Harry then back at Brent and asked, "Do you and Harry do UC work together? "No Harry's retired on duty. He's kind of burned out. He's recently divorced and has a bunch of girlfriends keeping him busy. He's a good guy, he'd do anything for you. I think his girlfriends are wearing him out."

Rene and Harry rejoined Brent and Val. The visit was good and the four drank a lot of beer.

As Brent got out of bed the next morning, he searched for a bottle of aspirin to relieve the hangover. Brent thought of the conversation he and Val had the night before. Working in Narcotics seemed like a good idea. The thought of getting back out on the streets sounded good. Brent made up his mind, today he was going to make narcotics his first choice on the transfer request.

Two weeks later, Brent walked into the homicide office with his stomach tied in knots. I hope I don't get punished for requesting a transfer. It will feel like punishment if I'm not transferred to another office.

Brent walked into the office and walked straight to the bulletin board. The transfer list for the entire department was posted. Looking over the list using his right index finger as a guide, he finally found his name, "Brent Mason from Homicide to Narcotics."

Involuntarily, a joyous little sound came from Brent's mouth. He was a little embarrassed and looked around to see if anyone heard him. Three of his coworkers were watching him because he was the only detective looking at the transfer list. Brent smiled politely at the current, about to be former, coworkers. He didn't want to act so happy, concerned someone might think he was leaving because he didn't like the people there.

He liked pretty much everyone and knew homicide was an important part of the department. But it just didn't suit him. Brent is a jeans and boots wearing kind of guy. The kind of guy that needed to get back out on the streets more.

Brent looked forward to the next chapter of his career with great anticipation and excitement. Then thought, I hope my wife doesn't have a fit about the transfer.

Chapter 4 Three Out of Five

Brent looked at the clock on his living room wall...again. He got out of bed at six after tossing and turning all night, anxious about his first day at narcotics. Brent thought starting the day at 2 pm is going to be different than starting at 7:30 in the morning. Feeling restless, he figured he'd just take care of a few things around the house and make the usual 20-minute commute drag into an hour, just to get on the road and get a start in his new office.

Brent walked into the narcotics office at 1:30. He figured it would show he was excited and ready to work. As he walked into the office, he saw an open bay area with desks grouped in clusters of four. There were doors on the walls surrounding the desks. The doors were to the sergeants' offices. Only one of the doors was open. Brent could hear a talk show radio host. He approached the door and saw a small plate attached to the door at eye level. The sign read, Sergeant Clower.

He walked in knowing Sgt. Clower was his new boss. Brent stood at the door outside of the office and knocked twice then waited for a response. He heard, "Come in." Brent walked in to see a large white man about 60 years old sitting behind the desk. He was taken aback by the lack of momentos and "I Love Me" plaques and certificates that adorned the walls of other supervisor's offices throughout the department. There was only one plaque centered on the wall behind the sergeant's desk. It read, "SAPD Patrolman of the Year, 1967", Brent thought wow, that's ten years before he had graduated from high school. The man stood from his chair, leaned forward over the desk, stuck out was right hand and said, "I'm Donnie Clower. You must be Brent."

Shaking his sergeants' hand, Brent smiled and said, "Yes sir, I am and I'm glad to be here."

The old crusty veteran said, "Have a seat Brent, let's talk a minute."

Brent wanted to be on his best behavior meeting his new boss and replied, "Yes sir, thank you sir." He reminded himself not to slouch or show any signs of disrespect during this first meeting.

"Brent, do you know any of the guys here?" asked Sgt Clower.

"Just Val and Harry, I met them a couple of weeks ago" replied Brent."

Clower continued, "You did? Did you meet them in a beer joint? That's usually the kind of place they make friends. They're very sociable in that setting."

After thinking for a second, Brent responded, "No sir, I think I met them at the headquarters building. A guy I used to work with introduced us."

Sgt. Clower leaned back in his chair grinned and said, "Brent, if you're going to work in this office, you have to learn to lie a lot better than that. You're never going to make an undercover case if you can't lie to somebody and convince them you're telling the truth."

Brent thought, damn, I've been in the office for only ten minutes and the Sgt has called me a liar. What a spectacular beginning. He wasn't sure what to say about the sergeant's remark, so he didn't say anything.

Sgt. Clower asked, "Have you thought about whether or not you want to do undercover work?"

"Well I don't know much about the office yet, but I guess I thought undercover work, is narcotics work," replied Brent.

Clower explained, "No, actually, Val is the only guy we've got that does UC work. Harry is supposed to make UC cases, but he's been slacking off lately. He used to be really good at it. I think the newly divorced lifestyle is getting the best of him. Most of the detectives here run search warrants based on information they get from an informant. Or, they might do a street arrest/pop if they get information on a guy selling dope on the street. Mingo does search warrants and street pops. I'm going to have you ride with him for a while. When you get a working understanding about what Mingo does, you'll ride with Val and do some UC stuff.

Brent replied, "Yes sir, that sounds great."

Sgt Clower started going over the basics of the job, "Brent, I'm going to give you a speech my sergeant gave me about 25 years ago, when I got here as a detective. This job can be a lot of fun, but it's full of pitfalls. If you're here very long, you're going to be put in positions where you need to be very careful. You'll be dealing with money, dope and informants. Mishandling any one of the three could land you in federal prison. The risks of not being careful with the money and dope are obvious. But, the risks with the CI's (Confidential Informants) is a little more obscure.

Some of the CI's have been providing detectives with information for years. They're master manipulators. It's extremely important for you to pay very close attention to the way Val and Mingo handle their informants. The informants are money motivated. Sometimes they'll try to get you to do something that isn't quite right or legal. They hope you'll find dope on something they're guessing about, and they'll get paid. Lucky for them. Occasionally, you'll be working in a gray area and the line isn't easy to see. Once you start doing UC buys, you have to get a good ID on your crook. If you don't, you might indict the wrong person. It becomes a big deal if you end up indicting the wrong person. They can be arrested for something they didn't do, and it reflects poorly on the department and the officer who is making the charge. When you start running search warrants it's important to be sure your hitting the right house. I know it sounds silly to think you could hit the wrong house, but it happens. After it gets dark out there things just don't look the same. When you add the normal stress of executing a warrant, or the stress of running a high-risk warrant, it happens. Hit the wrong house, indict the wrong person and you've got problems. I guess what I'm telling you is, be careful. Think things through before you act. Don't let enthusiasm get the best of you. Just be smart about all the things you do, and you'll be fine."

Brent thought that was a lot to take in on the first meeting with the new boss, but he kept telling himself that anything would be better than working all those assault cases.

The Sgt then asked, "Do you know Mingo Green?"

"No sir, I don't," replied Brent.

Clower continued, "Well, he's pretty easy to get along with. He'll probably have you doing some of his dirty work. He's big on street pops. He might have you running down some crooks. When I say running down, I mean a foot chase. Do you know what a street pop is?"

Brent did not want to show his inexperience but also wanted to make sure the Sgt didn't catch him in another lie, and replied, "No sir, I don't."

Sgt Clower explained that a street pop is when you get information on a street dealer and then you go out and pop him. It's a simple process except for the dealers who fight trying to get away, or the ones who choose to run. The Sgt then said, "You're a pretty big boy, I think you'll do alright if your hearts in it. I got a feeling Mingo's going to have you chasing some dopers. He used to chase them before he got old and fat. But don't let his age and pot belly fool you, he's still a scrapper. If you have any trouble, he'll be right in the middle of it with you."'

Brent told his new boss, "Sarge, I'm ready to get back on the streets. I'll do a good job here. I'll do what it takes to get the job done. I don't know if you asked anyone about it, but I did a pretty good job in homicide, and I didn't even like it there."

Sgt Clower replied, "Good, I'm glad to hear it. Why don't you wait out in the bay, the other guys will be here soon. I hope you're hungry, they like to go eat first thing."

"Yes sir, thank you" replied Brent, breathing a sigh of relief feeling that his first meeting with his new boss went better than he had been keeping himself awake over the previous night.

Brent walked back out into the office bay. He stood there looking around at how different it was than the homicide office. There weren't any short walls. It's better already he thought to himself. He walked around looking at some of the posters on the walls. Some were profane. There were five posters from the movie "Scarface". Another one of the posters said, "Don't screw with me, I screw back." Another read, "Got Meth? "He thought about how this was in such stark contrast from the almost empty walled office of the man in charge.

At five till two, Brent's new co-workers walked in laughing and joking with each other. Val, Mingo, Harry and Jimmy welcomed Brent with a big smile and handshake. Brent no longer felt nervous about his first day. He didn't even know these guy's and they've already made him feel at home.

Sgt. Clower walked out of his office for roll call. Roll call just amounted to making sure the guys scheduled to work were there. Sgt.Clower looked at Mingo and said, "Brent's going to ride with you."

Mingo replied, "That's great, I'm sure I can find something for him to do."

"I kind of figured that Mingo. I've already mentioned a few things to him about what you might find for him to do." said the Sgt.

Shortly after roll call, the day's first heated debate began. Most of the offices are the same way. During the shift an officer may have to make a decision that determines whether he will live or die. He may have to decide how best to handle a dangerous crook. But no decision will be more controversial than the answer to an important question,

"Where are we going to eat?" The men decide on a little Mexican restaurant near the office.

The five men entered the restaurant and were seated around a small table. Almost immediately a waitress met them at the table with four iced teas. Two sweet, and two unsweetened. She then looked at Mingo and asked, "Who's the new guy?"

Mingo answered, "Just call him new guy for now. I don't know how long he'll be here. I don't want you to get used to him just to find out he got scared and ran off to school services, or check fraud, or something less scary."

The waitress shook her finger at Mingo and said, "You behave old man. You were a new guy too once. Of course, that was a long, long time ago, probably when the dinosaurs roamed the planet."

All but Mingo enjoyed the waitress's statement.

Lunch was eaten faster than the time it took to get the food to get to the table. Mingo was ready to take Brent out to do some work. Mingo wiped his mouth and stood up from the table with Brent jumping up as quickly as he could. Mingo looked at the guys still seated and said, "We'll see you chumps later. We got some work to do.

The men still seated at the table didn't even look up and Jimmy responded, "Whatever Pops, be careful."

As Mingo drove out of the parking lot with Brent in the passenger seat, Mingo asked, "Well, are you ready to become a narc?"

"You better believe it. The sooner the better!", replied Brent

As Mingo drove toward the west side of San Antonio, he said, "I got a call today from an informant. He said there's a guy in the Apache Courts low income housing development selling dime bags of heroin out of his mouth. The heroin is in little party balloons. Have you ever been in the Apaches?"

Brent replied, "Yeah, I worked the west side for five years. I've made a few little dope cases there, but it was usually just luck. I chased down a few guys and found a little in their pocket."

Mingo interjected, "Narcotics work isn't rocket science, Brent. The main thing is you have to be willing to do the work. It's going to be more physical than what you had in homicide. But, if your hearts in it you'll be fine."

Brent thought to himself most everyone around him continues to use the phrase, "If your hearts in it", he never heard that phrase for the whole time he was in homicide. He told Mingo, "I'm not afraid of the physical part, if that's what you're wondering." "That's good. A lot of guys have transferred into this office and found out pretty quickly it wasn't for them. Have you ever done a street pop before?"

Brent thought, Damn I'm glad Sgt. Clower told me about street pops an hour ago. "Not really, like I said, there's been a time or two I kind of made a case by accident."

Mingo said, "Well this time you're going to do it on purpose. When we get to the courts, I'll start looking for the guy my boy told me about. I'm not sure what the crooks wearing, but I'll know him when I see him. When I pick him out, I'll get you as close to him as I can in the car. He'll probably spook and run. When he runs, we'll know we've got the right guy. Then, you jump out and chase him down. Have you ever choked a street dealer to get his dope?"

Brent replied, "No, this will be a new experience for me."

Mingo shrugged a little and said, "I have to admit, it takes a little getting used too. Putting your hand around a man's throat and choking him doesn't come naturally. Not unless you're really pissed off. Just remember, it's only business. It's nothing personal. Dopers expect to get choked out once in a while. They won't hold it against you. It's considered an occupational hazard."

Concerned about a force complaint, Brent tentatively asked, "Uh, what if I choke him out and he doesn't have anything?"

Mingo appeared to become irritated and said, "If he runs, he's got a mouth full of balloons. Sometimes they just beat you and get the balloons swallowed before you get a good grip on them. Like I told you, if they're dealing out of their mouth, they expect to get choked occasionally. If they wanted to avoid it, they'd keep the dope in their pocket. But then again, that would make it easier for us to make a case on them. They'd rather risk getting choked. That way they have a better chance to swallow it and avoid getting arrested. They were doing it that way when I started twenty years ago. The old timers told me they were doing it that way when they started. Don't worry about it. You'll get to liking it after you've done it a few times. I used to love it. I'm sure I would still love it, but I can't catch them anymore. That's why Clower put you with me."

As Mingo drove his maroon Malibu through the courts, he looked from side to side, then looking straight ahead Mingo said, "Get ready, he's in here somewhere."

Brent placed his right hand on the door handle ready to bail out. Brent said, "I feel like a bird dog about to flush a covey of quail."

Mingo laughed at the comment and replied, "Yeah well, when I say sick-em, you jump out, catch him and choke the shit out of this quail. There he is, get ready!"

A Hispanic man about 25 years old was walking on the sidewalk. Mingo said, "I'm pretty sure that's him. Let's see if he'll spook."

Mingo hit the gas. The engine roared, and he drove straight at the man. The guy looked back with eyes as big as saucers. As Mingo brought the car to a sliding stop, the man broke and ran toward the apartments. Mingo screamed, "Get him, Brent!"

Brent jumped out of the car and the chase was on. Even though he was about seven years older than the suspect, he was quickly closing in.

Mingo got out of the car and was cheering Brent on screaming over and over, "Get him, Brent", between laughs as he walked slowly toward the action.

Just about the time Mingo screamed the fourth time, the chase ended with a horse collar tackle. A huge cloud of dust came up where the two hit the ground.

Brent remembered his instructions and as unnatural as it seemed, rolled the guy over and grabbed him by the throat. Brent said calmly to the man, "Boy, I sure hope you've got something."

Mingo caught up and leaned over the pile. He stood just to the side as Brent sat on the man's chest with his right hand firmly on the man's throat. Mingo leaned over placing his hands on his knees and said, "Spit 'em out son, and he'll let go."

Just as Brent was worrying about what Mingo got him into, the suspect used his tongue to push 15 multi-colored balloons from his mouth. As the balloons were coming out, Mingo started a celebration yelling, "All right, way to go, Brent."

Through heavy breathing, Brent asked Mingo, "You got any cuffs?"

"Yeah, I figured you'd forget that part", replied Mingo.

Brent and Mingo booked their prisoner back at the station, did the paperwork and were out of the jail in about an hour. Mingo looked at his watch as they drove through the parking lot and said, "An hour spent on lunch, and two hours catching and booking a prisoner. I'd call that a damn good day. Yes, Sir Brent, I think you're going to work out just fine."

Brent leaned back in the passenger seat eating up the praise and thought, "Now that's real police work."

As they drove away from the jail, Brent asked, "What are we going to do now, Mingo?"

The old crusty veteran, proud of the work done on his rookies' first day on the street as a narcotics officer asked, "Do you drink beer?"

Brent thought it was an odd question but answered, "Uh, yeah, I do."

To which Mingo replied, "Well then we're gonna go drink beer."

They ended up at one of Mingo's favorite places. It was a little beer joint surrounded by picnic tables. The tables were strategically placed under big live oak trees. There was no food to speak of, unless you consider pickled quail's eggs and beef jerky food. They picked up two beers each at the front of the beer joint and turned to find just the right table under the trees.

They sat their beers on the table and took a seat.

Brent said, "I like this place. It reminds me of where my dad and uncle used to take me. I would play pool, or shuffle board as they drank beer. I liked picking out songs on the jukebox."

Mingo asked, "Did you grow up in San Antonio?"

"Yeah, I grew up on the south side.", replied Brent.

Mingo asked again, "You grew up on the south side? You got a pretty deep tan, but you don't look Mexican."

Brent replied, "I'm not, I think there were two other white families on the block. I guess you could say I'm fully assimilated. My buddies and girlfriends taught me a little Spanish. What about you, your darker than me and Domingo Green is kind of a funny name. It seems you'd be as comfortable at a conjunto festival as you would at the rodeo."

Mingo opened up to Brent and said, "Well I wasn't born Domingo Green, I was born Domingo Martinez. My worthless ass old man ran off from me and my mom when I was eight. We ended up in the courts, just like the ones we were in today. We were there three years when my mom met a man named Green. They got married and he got us out of the courts. He was really good to us. He asked me a time or two if I wanted to be adopted and take his name. I guess I didn't like the idea. I don't know why. I liked him and he saved me and my mom from poverty. One day he came to pick me up from freshman football practice and one of my friends called him Mr. Martinez. It kind of freaked me out. I thought he would correct the kid, but he didn't. He just went right on talking to the kid and didn't even flinch. I thought about it for about a month. I decided if he was willing to be called by my name, I should be willing to be called by his. He adopted me about a week later."

Brent opened his eyes wide and said, "Wow, that's one hell of a story. Did you ever hear from Martinez again?"

Mingo replied, "Yeah he showed up at my house after I was married and had two kids. He said he was sorry and wanted to be a part of my life now. I told him, I don't need you now. I needed you when we were broke and in the courts. I told that old son of a bitch, why don't you go back and crawl under that rock you came out of."

Mingo asked Brent, "Have you been on the department long?"

Brent replied, "No, I almost got hired in 1983 when I was twenty-two. I was disqualified under the old back requirement. They used to give back x-rays and if they found anything at all, no matter how small, you'd be disqualified. The city was using guidelines written by the Southern Pacific Railroad in 1924."

Mingo questioned, "1924, that's hard to believe. Are you telling me the city hadn't changed the physical guidelines from 1924?"

Brent replied, "Yes, and they wouldn't have changed them then, but a person rejected just like me filed a lawsuit. That put the city on the wrong end of yet another lawsuit. That seems to happen regularly. Rather than pay the guy, they changed the guideline. When I applied again in 1990, there was no back x-ray and I got hired. And aren't you glad Mingo? If I hadn't been hired, who would be catching crooks for you?"

Mingo, "Oh, I agree, Brent. I'm glad you're here. It was a lot easier for me to get in the department. I was selling shoes at Tom McCann in '75. A buddy of mine stopped in for a pair of shoes and told me he was going to take the police department test. He asked me if I wanted to go with them. I didn't even own a car. I walked out of Tom McCann, went to take the test and a month later I was a policeman. I've never given it much thought, but I'm glad that old boy came in that morning. "

The next few days went just like the first. An hour for lunch, two hours to catch and process a crook, then drinking beer. Man, what a great job! Professional fun followed by a cold beer. Brent thought It just don't get no better than this. Three days in the narcotics office and three street dealers were in jail.

The fourth time Brent and Mingo went cruising the courts for one of Mingo's suspects, they drove up on two guys talking at a street corner. One of the young men was holding a bike in front of him.

Mingo stopped his car about 20 yards from where the two guys were standing and said to Brent, "I'm not sure which one is holding. I'll run the car at them, and you get the one that spooks." Mingo sped the car toward the two frightened men on the corner. Both men seemed terrified, but neither one moved. Brent looked at Mingo and asked, "Well, which one?"

Mingo exclaimed, "Get the one with the bike!" Brent jumped out of the car and bum rushed the guy holding the bike. The bike didn't slow him down. He just ran through the middle of the bike and grabbed the man by the throat.

Brent said, "Spit 'em out." Barely audible the man opened his mouth wide and said, "I ain't got nothin'." Brent closely looked around in the man's open mouth and sure enough, no balloons.

It only took Brent a few seconds to think, this is exactly what I was afraid of. I knocked the guy off his feet, broke his bike, and probably dinged him up a little and there's no dope. He thought, "I'll probably be suspended for a week over this."

Mingo was quickly standing next to Brent who was helping their suspect off the ground. Brent had a nervous look. Mingo could see the concern on Brent's face, in his body language and his silence. Mingo spoke up boldly to their suspect. "Hey look here asshole. You just beat us today that's all. I know you swallowed those balloons. We'll catch you next time. Come on Brent, let's go!"

As they walked to the car, Mingo tried to reassure Brent. He patted him on the back a couple of times and said, "Hey, don't worry about it. He just swallowed on us, that's all." With his hand still on Brent's back he led Brent to the car. After opening the car door, Brent looked back to see their, "Suspect", examining his bent-up bike frame and scrapes and scratches on his arms and legs.

Mingo could clearly see Brent was bothered by the day's events. Mingo said, "Hey you know what, we've had a pretty good week. Why don't we call it a day?"

They drove to their favorite drinking spot for a few beers. They sat quietly for the first few minutes and didn't make eye contact. Mingo broke the silence and said, "Hey, don't worry about it, he's a dealer. He just beat us. I've seen the same thing that happened today a hundred times. He's not going to complain. What's he going to do, walk in to

Internal Affairs and tell them, I was dealing heroin out of my mouth today and some guys knocked me down.

Sometimes you get the bear and sometimes the bear gets you."

Pretty much the same scenario played out the next day. As they cruised the projects looking for another one of Mingo's, "Suspects", Brent wasn't quite as anxious to tackle and choke another target. He was still thinking about the guy that just, "Beat them."

After cruising the courts for a few minutes, Mingo spotted his target and pointed him out to Brent. As Mingo pointed, he said, "Get him, Brent!"

Brent jumped out of the car and ran toward the suspect. When Brent got within a few steps of him, the suspect opened his mouth as wide as he could and raised both open hands in the air.

Brent stopped in his tracks. Judging by what happened the day before, it was clear Mingo's, "Suspect", had nothing in his mouth, or hands.

Brent didn't even make contact with the man. He stood in front of the suspect for a few seconds thinking about what just happened and the proverbial light in his head came on.

Brent was fuming. His face was red, and he was breathing heavily. He walked slowly back toward Mingo as Mingo stood behind the open driver's side door. Mingo had a worried look on his face. Mingo had seen the kind of physical activity Brent was capable of. Brent stopped just shy of the driver's side door in front of Mingo. Brent yelled, "Mingo you bastard, your guessing, aren't you?"

Mingo smiled, shrugged his shoulders and said, "Hey man, three out of five ain't bad."

Chapter 5 The First Buy

Six months after being welcomed to the office, management decided to assign Bent to ride with Val.

At the beginning of the day, Sgt. Clower walked into the conference room to hold roll call. He took a long slow look to see if all his detectives were there. He looked at Val and said, "I think Brent has a pretty good grasp on the warrants and street pops (arrests). I want him to ride with you. Besides, I think he's been carrying Mingo's load long enough. He told me he wants to do some undercover (UC) stuff. I want you to show him how it's done. "

The sergeant looked at Brent and said, "Brent, you're in good hands. Val is the best UC man there ever was."

The sergeant's praises for Val brought cheers and whistles from the others. Val looked at Sgt. Clower and said, "Hey thanks sarge. How about a raise?"

Clower replied, "Oh, I wish I could Val, but all I can do is blow a little smoke. But I want you to know, I'm sincere about the smoke I'm blowin'. Unfortunately, that's all I have to offer you."

Val said, "I'll take it. I really could use some help with the UC work. Just like Brent was carrying Mingo's load, I've been carrying the UC load by myself long enough." Looking over at Harry who was sitting at his desk on the phone as usual, Val said, "There used to be a guy around here that would help me out. I haven't seen him lately. I wonder what ever happened to that ole boy?" There was a group laugh at Harry's expense.

Val looked at Brent and said, "We'll start today. I know just the place to take you. It's a dime house on the Westside. It's been in business for about twenty or thirty years. It's not like the place is a secret.

Search warrants are done there about once a month. The tecatos dealing there get arrested and the next day another junkie is slinging dimes. The names change, but the activity remains the same."

Val continued, "Reggie took me there for my first buy and that was twelve years ago. Now I'm going to take you there. I guess we might as well make it a tradition. Maybe someday you'll take a guy there for his first buy. Are you up for it?"

Brent didn't want to sound too eager out loud, but in a restrained voice said, "You bet Val. I'm ready. I don't know what I'm going to do or say. I figure you'll clue me in on that."

Val said, "Well boys, let's go have some lunch. After that, Brent and I will leave you loafers and get some work done."

After arriving at their favorite Mexican food restaurant. Each member of the group took their turn ordering lunch. When it was Jimmy's turn, he asked the waitress, "Can you put my tacos on one plate and my rice and beans on separate plates?" The waitress looked at Jimmy for a second then scanned the faces of the others and said, "Sure Jimmy, I can do that." Then she rolled her eyes and walked away. As the waitress left, Mingo looked at Jimmy and said, "You're killin' me with that stupid crap. Put my tacos on one plate, and my rice and beans on separate plates. What the hell is wrong with you? Are you freakin' nuts?"

Jimmy replied, "No Mingo, there's nothing wrong with me. I just don't like all of my food touching. What's wrong with that? Is that so strange?" To which Mingo replied, "Yeah, it's strange. It's very strange. As a matter of fact, I think you need to go see a shrink. "

Val chimed in, "I hate to get in the middle of this, but I think he's right Jimmy. You really should go talk to a psychiatrist. You're the only person I have ever seen in my life that orders like that. It's just not normal."

Jimmy told the group in a loud voice, "I don't need a shrink. Some people might think I'm crazy, but not because of my food. They might think I'm crazy because of the people I hang out with. What's it to you guys, anyway?" Mingo said, "I'll tell you what's wrong with me. The way you order embarrasses the hell out of me. What do you think about the way people feel when we're sitting with you? They probably think we're crazy too."

After a few seconds of silence, Brent asked Jimmy, "Do you eat hotdogs?" "Yeah, I eat hotdogs, Brent. What are you getting at?" replied Jimmy.

Mingo answered, "I'll tell you what he's getting at. He's trying to figure out why a guy that doesn't want his beans and rice touching his tacos would eat something like a hotdog. When you get a hotdog, cow's eyeballs are touching a pig's asshole!"

Jimmy leaned back in his chair, threw his hands in the air and yelled, "Oh, you think you're so smart. I know enough about assholes to know there's four big ones sitting at this table!"

After lunch, Brent and Val drove away from the restaurant in Val's green T-bird. They were headed to the old house Val mentioned has been slinging dimes of heroin for decades. During the trip, Brent sat quietly on the passenger side. Val could see he was uneasy.

Val asked, "Are you nervous, Brent?"

"Yeah, I guess a little," replied Brent, trying to cover the knots in his stomach.

Val smiled and said, "That's normal. Don't worry about it. It's understandable when you are doing something new. I don't think it's about making a drug buy. I think it's about doing something different. Weren't you a little nervous when you got to homicide? I mean, you hadn't worked a murder case before."

Brent replied, "I guess I was."

Val trying to be comforting said, "You see it's normal. You're going to be fine. Do you know how I'm sure you'll be fine?"

"No, how?" asked Brent.

Val said, "Because you're willing to try. A lot of guys have come to this office thinking they were going to be the next big UC man. But when it came down to making their first buy, they didn't have the nerve for it. That's the hardest part. Walking into the unknown. Most of the time when it doesn't go well all we're talking about is not getting the buy down. You're more likely to get hurt running a search warrant than you are on a $10 dime bag buy."

Brent told Val, "I'm not really worried about getting hurt. I'm more worried about it not working out. Mingo already told me I'll never be able to do UC work. He says, dopers will never sell to me and that I look to much like a cop. He says I might as well be wearing a uniform. If I don't get the buy made, I'll never hear the end of it. I can hear him now saying, I told you so. I told you so."

Val could sense Brent's anxiety building and said, "Mingo doesn't know what the hell he's talking about. He's never made of buy in his life. He doesn't know there isn't a look for a buyer. People that buy dope come in all shapes and sizes. Some have money and some don't. Some guys trying to do this kind of work think they have to dress up in some sort of costume. They think they have to put a bandana on their head and wear old work clothes. It doesn't make any sense to me. Why would you want to show up looking like you don't have any money? If I was selling dope, I would want customer's that looked like they have money. I'd rather deal with a guy that wanted a hundred dollars' worth, rather than ten different guys buying ten separate dimes."

Brent thought of the sage advice Val offered and replied, "I hadn't thought about it that way, Val. I guess I thought there was a look too."

Val continued, "It's not about how you dress. It's about how you act. If you look nervous or say the wrong thing, they might turn you down. Act like you would if you were out buying a TV or even placing an order at a fast food drive in. Keep the personality out of the conversation and just stick to business"

Val pulled into the parking lot of a, "Mom and Pop" convenience store. He told Brent, "I'll be right back."

Val walked out of the store and returned to the car with two large paper bags. He handed one to Brent.

Brent looked in his bag and saw Val bought two quarts of beer. Val said, "Take a couple of big swigs of that. It'll calm your nerves."

Brent folded down the sides of the bag so he could twist the top off the bottle, took a big drink and said, "Damn, that's pretty good."

As they drove toward the dime house, Val handed Brent a twenty-dollar bill and told him, "Take this, the sarge gave me buy money last week. When you get to the door, tell the guy you want two dimes of brown. He'll know what you're talking about. I wouldn't want you to go to your first buy and say, excuse me sir, I would like to purchase $20 worth of heroin if you don't mind."

Brent laughed and said, "Oh, thanks. I've never made a buy before, but I'm hoping I wouldn't have said it like that."

Val drove up in front of a small house with windows surrounded by burglar bars. He parked on the curb that was only about twenty feet from the door. Val said, "The guy will probably crack the door a little and ask you what you want. He'll probably stand back where you can't see him. They think it will keep them from getting charged with a delivery if they can't be identified. Get as good a look as you can. Try to see a tattoo or other identifying mark and make sure to remember what kind of clothing he's wearing. When he hands you the dope, get a look at his hands. You might see a ring or something. Try to come away with something we can give Mingo for an ID. We'll get him to run a warrant later. Go on now, go to the door and make your first buy."

As Brent left the car he had to chuckle inside as the advice offered strangely reminded him of the instructions given to him by his parents on his first days of going to school on what to do and what not to do. Brent walked to the front door and knocked. A few seconds later the door opened a few inches. The front door was also behind burglar bars. Brent couldn't see who opened the door. He heard a man's voice just inside the door. The man asked, "Que queres?" Brent thought, oh no, this little buy operation has already gone to shit. He didn't consider the conversation with a prospective dealer might be in Spanish. With a stupid look on his face, Brent turned to look at Val in the car. The car was close enough for Val to hear what was being said. Val told Brent, "He's asking you what you want."

Brent looked back to the slightly open door and said, "Two dimes."

The man behind the door then asked, "De que?" Once again Brent didn't understand what he was saying. Brent looked back at Val and Val said, "He's asking you, of what."

Looking at the door again Brent said, "Of brown."

The man then said, "Dome la dinero", which means "Give me the money."

Brent turned to look at Val again. Apparently, the man behind the door was tired of the three-way conversation and yelled, "Oh, just give me the money man."

Brent stuck a twenty-dollar bill through the burglar bars, and into the small opening of the door. The unknown man handed Brent, two small party balloons. Brent told the man what he thought was appropriate said, "Gracious" which was a terrible version of "Gracias".

The man behind the door said, "Oh, whatever dude."

Brent got back in the car and Val drove away laughing hysterically.

Val said, "Well, it isn't the smoothest buy I've ever seen, but you got the dope. That's the main thing.

I can see I'm going to have to give you some Spanish you can use in a situation like that."

As Val and Brent got out of the car in the office parking lot, Brent asked, "You're not going to tell anybody about this, are you? You know I attended a predominantly Hispanic high school and I knew what the seller was saying. But for some reason, my mind just got stuck on don't screw this up. I had a brain fart. I temporarily went blank on all the Spanish I know."

Still laughing Val said, "Hell, yes I am. The first thing I'm going to do when we get in the office is tell Mingo."

"Don't do that Val. That's exactly what I was worried about", replied Brent.

The laughter wore off and there were a few silent miles as they made their way back to the station when Val asked, "Brent, do you really expect me to keep this to myself?"

"Yes, I do" replied Brent, not wanting to be the target of the hazing he knew he would endure with the disclosure that Brent couldn't even answer the basic questions the seller was asking in Spanish.

As Val and Brent walked back into the office, Brent's head was hanging down anticipating the grief he was about to get. The first thing they heard was Mingo, "Well, did he score?" Worried about what Val might say, Brent kept his mouth shut and stared at the floor. Val answered, "Boy, do I have a story for you." Brent sat down, placed his elbows on his desk and put his head in his hands.

Brent thought, this thing is going to follow me around for the rest of my life.

Val looked at Brent as he told the expanding group of detectives, "That was the smoothest first buy I've ever seen. You would think Brent has done it a hundred times before."

Stunned by what Val said, Brent looked up at Val and put a big smile on his face.

Val and Brent laughed. The assembled gaggle of veteran narcs had confused looks on their faces. They knew something happened out there, but they also knew neither Val or Brent would ever tell.

Chapter 6 The Quiet Truck

Brent and Mingo met at a driving range near the office to hit a bucket of balls before work. As Brent set another ball on the ground, he looked at Mingo and said, "I think November is my favorite time of year down here in South Texas. I just feel better when it's cool like this. Highs in the seventies and lows in the fifties, how can you beat that? I think the worst month of the year is August. Except for my birth day, I don't know of anything else good about August."

Mingo leaned on his golf club and said, "Oh, I agree. Trying to get something done in the summer is brutal. You know, even my dogs feel better in November than they do in August. It's also the best time of year for fishing at the coast. I wish they would build a golf course in Rockport. It would be great to fish in the morning and golf in the afternoon. I could put my clubs in the car. I love the thought of launching my little boat at daylight catching a few fish, and then straight to golf after the filets are in the ice chest."

Brent agreed, "I think the best fishing trips I've ever had was on Estes Flats in November. One time, Dahlen and I were catching redfish so fast and so easy, we would clean one limit, put them in an ice chest and go catch another limit. We did that for three days in a row."

Mingo said, "Your lucky you didn't get caught. With my luck there would have been a game warden waiting for me when I got back to the ramp with the second limit."

"We almost did get caught the third day. I was sure Dahlen was going to cause it."

Mingo laughed and asked, "Your brother in law almost caused you to get tickets? How did he do that?"

"We were standing at the cleaning table with the second stringer of redfish and a game warden drove up. There was a little café near the boat ramp we used. I think he was just there to get a hamburger. He parked and looked over at us standing there cleaning fish. I knew it would be a bad idea not to speak to him, so I put on a big smile and waved. He asked, did ya'll do any good? Still with the biggest smile I had I said, we did great. We caught our limit so fast, we're going home early. I think I'll cut the grass. He said, boy that's good, you must be lucky. I thought to myself, lucky, it looks to me like our luck may have just run out."

While I was doing my best to not look guilty, Dahlen was still cleaning fish and didn't see the warden. With his back turned to the warden he asked me, who is that, do you know him? I told him don't look, a game warden just drove up. And what did that dumb ass do, he turned to look. I quietly said, didn't I just tell you not to look? He turned back to the table, but he was acting guilty as hell. All the time I spent acting not guilty, Dahlen was trying to get us caught by acting guilty."

As Mingo laughed, he asked, "So what happened, did he write y'all a ticket?

"No, I turned around to put fillets in the ice chest and saw the warden walking to the café. Man, I'm glad he didn't see the way my brother in law was acting. He would have written us tickets for sure."

At about noon the other members of the group were getting ready for work. Most live less than an hour away from the office. Val got a phone call from a very reliable informant. Val answered the phone and heard, "Hey Val, it's Raymond."

In a surprised reaction Val said, "Hi Raymond, what's going on?" Raymond was very excitable and always on a mission to get paid for information said, "Val, one of the guys I know is bringing a load of heroin from Mexico. I know he's on the way back from Eagle Pass right now." Val pressed Raymond, "Do you know where he is, Raymond? I mean, is he getting close to San Antonio?"

Raymond replied, "No, he's still a long way off. I know the route he's taking though. He's bragged about it to me before. He says he crosses at Eagle Pass, then drives onto a ranch before the checkpoint. He says he has to drive dirt roads for about an hour, and that once he comes back onto FM 59, he's past the checkpoint. He said the traffickers bought the ranch to have a way around the checkpoint. I just got off the phone with him. He just got through the gate on the ranch."

Val was skeptical, "Raymond, why would this guy tell you all about what he's doing? It doesn't really make sense. Why would he tell you about the drive? Does he want to get arrested or something?"

Raymond was getting more agitated as the conversation continued, "Val, I'm telling you, he's coming back right now with a load. He tells me all the stuff because he wants me to know how important and smart, he is. He thinks he's got the cops outsmarted. He's told me a hundred times he'll never get caught. He thinks he's smarter than ya'll."

Trying to placate Raymond, Val continued, "Okay, so the guy is still east of Eagle Pass. That means we have plenty of time to get down there. But how are we going to find this guy on the highway in all that traffic? That drive is at least sixty miles from the intersection to San Antonio."

Raymond laughed and said, "It won't be hard to find him. He's in a yellow Ford pickup with black rims. The damn thing looks like a bumblebee going down the road. You'll be able to see it a mile off."

Val was still on the phone and was thinking out loud and said, "If he just got on to the ranch, he's still west of the checkpoint. He's probably about an hour away from Interstate 35. If I get the guys out now to IH 35 and FM 59. We should be there before him. "Okay Raymond, we'll give it a shot."

After hanging up with Raymond, Val pushed the press to talk button on his phone. When their phones beeped, each member of the group heard Val saying, "Hey, we need to pick up a truck at IH 35 and Highway 59 coming north from Eagle Pass. Did everybody copy?"

Val waited for a response while looking at his phone and heard Brent respond, "I got it, Val. Mingo and I are together, we're on the way." Jimmy said, "I got it too, Harry's with me, we're both on the way." "Ok, I'll see you at IH 35 and FM 59. Keep an eye out while you're driving south. Raymond says the truck were looking for is a yellow Ford with black rims. He says it looks like a giant bumblebee."

Val was waiting for them to arrive at the rendezvous point. He pulled into a truck stop near the intersection. As he drove through the parking lot toward the store, the site of a bright yellow pick up jumped out at him like it was made of neon. Val got back on the radio and said, "That was easy, I've got it here at the truck stop near the intersection. Is anyone else getting close?" Brent answered, "Yeah, I'm almost there, Val. I see Harry and Jimmy behind me. Will be there in about 15 minutes."

Val replied, "Why don't you just pull over on the northbound side of IH 35. It looks like Raymond's info was pretty good. I'm pretty sure he's got something. If he goes south, I'll let you know, and you can catch up."

A few minutes after Val entered the parking lot, he watched a man leave the store at the truck stop and get into a yellow truck. Val watched as the truck left the store and drove through the highway intersection. It was northbound on IH

35. Val told the guys, "I got him on the move, he's headed north on IH 35. You guys just stay where you are, we're coming your way." Mingo said, "Okay, we'll be here waiting." About 15 minutes later, the yellow truck and Val drove by the others parked on the side of the highway. Brent said, "We see you Val, we'll fall in behind you." Val replied, "Okay, let's just follow at a distance until we get to San Antonio. We'll get someone to help us with a stop after we get to the city limits."

An hour later as they were getting close to San Antonio, Val got back on the air and said, "Brent, do you think you can get us a traffic officer to make a stop?" Brent replied, "Yeah, I'm on it."

A few minutes later, Brent said, "Val, I got the patrolmen set up at Loop 410 and IH 35. He has a Department of Transportation certification and will play it off as an interdiction stop." Val asked, "That sounds great Brent, is he working on our channel?" Brent didn't have time to respond before the traffic officer replied, "Yeah, I'm over here. Just let me know when you want me to make the stop." Val directed, "Okay, let's stop it whenever you're ready after we're passed 410."

After the yellow truck drove over Hwy 90 on 410, the traffic officer fell in behind it and turned on his overhead lights. The yellow truck moved to the side of the highway and stopped. Val told the officer, "We'll come up and meet you after you get the driver out. Let's work it like an interdiction."

After the stop was made and the truck was safely off the highway, Val, Mingo and Brent walked up to the officer and the driver. The officer was checking the driver's license and insurance card. Val said to the driver, "Hi, I'm Detective Martinez with the San Antonio police narcotics unit. We are working interdiction on the highways. May I ask you where you're coming from?" The man said, "I'm just coming from Devine. I was visiting my grandmother. She's very sick and I took her some groceries. I had to fix a leak under her kitchen sink. She's feeling better and I think she's going to be fine."

Val said, "Well I'm glad to hear that. It's very nice of you to help your grandma. I'm sure she appreciates it. You're a good grandson. Look, I don't want to keep you very long, but do you mind if we go through your truck. It's just part of the stuff we're expected to do once in a while. It won't take long. It's just something we have to do to make sure no one is carrying guns or explosives, anything like that."

The driver replied somewhat assuredly, "No sir, I don't mind. You can check it all you want. I don't have anything to hide." Val replied, "Okay, that's great, it shouldn't take more than a few minutes. Would you mind standing with the officer on the side of the road?" "Sure, no problem." replied the driver.

The driver joined the officer outside the passenger side of the truck. Mingo and Brent searched the truck for a few minutes and found nothing unusual. Mingo looked at Val after not finding any contraband and asked, "How much are we looking for?" Val replied, "I don't know, Mingo. It could be a thousand pounds or an ounce. How the hell should I know?" "Take it easy, Val. I was just asking. Val calmed down a little and said, "I don't think he would be crossing the border with an ounce. I would think it's at least a kilo."

Mingo and Brent went back to searching the truck again. They looked under the seats, under the hood and in the tool box. They couldn't find anything. Mingo and Brent were about to give up and were standing at the back of the truck. Mingo lowered the tailgate and sat down, then said "Damn Val, you had us traveling all over South Texas on a wild goose chase. "

As Val rubbed his chin he said, "I don't know, Raymond seemed pretty sure about this one. It looks like everything he talked about. The guy's lying about where he's been. I think it's here somewhere, we just have to find it."

Mingo said, "Well, you boys wake me up when you're done." Then laid-back onto the bed of the pickup and placed his ball cap over his eyes. Brent was looking at Mingo with disgust. Then he noticed something odd about the end of the truck bed. The truck bed was black, and the end of the bed was black, but he noticed it was freshly painted. As he looked closer, he thought he could see new welds in the metal. Brent walked to this truck and opened his toolbox. He pulled out a cordless drill with a long bit attached. Brent walked to the right side of the truck bed and started drilling a hole in the bed. When Brent started drilling, Mingo was startled by the sound of a metal drill bit cutting into a metal truck bed.

Mingo jumped up from the bed of the truck and asked, "What the hell are you doing?" By the time Mingo got his question out, Brent was looking at the drill bit. Brent said, "I bet this truck rides very quietly."

That got Val's attention. Val asked, "Why do you say that?" Still looking at the drill bit Brent said, "There's black sticky stuff on this drill bit. It looks, and smells like tar heroin to me. I think the heroin is between the bed and the frame."

Val turned to the traffic officer and asked, "Would you mind putting him in the back of your car?

I think we're going to take this thing to the shop."
They had the yellow truck towed to the city auto shop. Mechanics used a pneumatic chisel to cut an opening in the truck bed. Fifteen kilos of tar heroin were recovered.

After the heroin was documented and placed into evidence, Brent looked at Mingo and said, "We couldn't have made this case without you. I think the chief is going to give you a medal."

Mingo said, "Your damn right you couldn't have done this without me. What did I do?"

Brent said, "Mingo, if your lazy ass wasn't laying in the bed of that truck, I never would have seen those welds. I can't tell you how many times I've heard somebody say your worthless. But I guess your good for something after all.

Chapter 7 Skinny Johnny Calls

It was 2 o'clock, on a hot South Texas Wednesday afternoon. The day started pretty much like any other. Val had his feet up on the desk and was working a crossword puzzle. Harry was in the same position on the other end of the office talking on the phone to one of his girlfriends. Brent was doing some paperwork related to a case he made earlier in the week. Mingo was intensely concentrating on his computer screen. He wasn't sure which move he should make next. He was involved in a very important game of solitaire. Jimmy was sitting at his desk, head hung low, quietly hoping his hangover would go away soon.

The silence was broken by the ringing of Brent's cell phone. He looked at the number on the incoming call and said, "Damn." The caller was one of his semi-regular informants. He stared at the caller ID trying to decide whether to answer. He didn't want to talk to him, but then again, he hated to think he might miss something. Skinny Johnny was a pain in the ass but occasionally he did have some pretty good information. Brent decided to answer and slapped the top of his desk with a loud bang. That startled the others in the group. Then he answered the phone and asked, "What do you want?"

Johnny replied, "Hey man, is that anyway talk to your main man? I got some killer info and you're dissin' me. I'm telling you Brent, this could be a big one."

Brent knew Johnny was predisposed to inflating all the information he gave and said, "Yeah, all right, I'm sorry. Let me start over. What the hell do you want?"

Johnny replied, "Uh, I guess that's a little better. Hey man, I know where some guys are going to be stashing a pile of weed." Brent rolled his eyes and asked, "How much is a pile? I mean is a pile one-pound, 10 pounds or a hundred pounds?" Johnny replied, "I'm not sure yet, but I was told to go rent a room at the Rainbow Motel downtown. They said they wanted me to get one of the bigger rooms. It sounds like it should be a lot of weed. The guy that told me to rent the room is a captain in the Mexican Mafia. He said, don't screw it up. The guys coming in are supposed to be related to the Hernandez cartel. I think it could be cartel -related because the mafia guy is no joke. He seemed pretty serious."

Brent was agitated by this information and said, "The Hernandez cartel, that doesn't make any sense. Why would they need a room to stash weed? A load of weed that can fit in a motel room doesn't sound like a lot of weed to me. They are crossing tons of weed at a time in tractor trailers. Their bull shittin' you. Your info must be screwed up. You're probably just saying it's a lot of weed because you want us to go out."

Johnny came up with his usual line, "Come on Brent, you know I wouldn't do you like that. I know you guys aren't usually interested in weed cases, but I'm broke. My family needs to eat. I could really use the info payment if it turns out. I'll tell you the truth man, I called one of the DEA guys with it, but he just talked crap to me. I thought he would be interested because it was supposed to be cartel related. Come on man, help me out, I'm broke."

Brent rolled his eyes and leaned back in his chair. Brent said, "Oh, so you called DEA first. You called DEA, they turned you down and then you called me. Why wasn't I the first one you thought of when you got this killer info?"

Johnny replied, "Come on Brent, you know why. They pay better than the city does. You can't hold it against me for trying to get top dollar, can you?"

Brent then said, "I hate to say it, but you do have a point. If the DEA isn't interested in a weed case, why should I be?"

Johnny then started his line of how the SAPD was better than the Feds, "Because you guys aren't lazy like they are. They want me to get the information, get the names of the crooks and write it down. They might as well give me a badge." To which Brent said, "I don't know Johnny, I was planning on typing all day. I might be able to get out later if I get some of this typing done. What time are they supposed to come in?" Johnny was then trying to press the issue, "I'm not sure, but I was told to get a room today and pay for it tomorrow. They told me someone would call me later and I should meet them at the corner of Houston and Frio to give them the key. They told me not to screw it up or it would be my ass."

Brent replied, "Yeah, all right. Call me when you pass off the key. We'll go check on it. You know weed cases don't pay much unless it's a pretty heavy weight."

Sensing that he had the score Johnny replied, "Yeah, I know, but if you do make a case, anything will help. I really appreciate it. I tell you what I'll do, the next time I get something good, I'll call you first. That's what the DEA gets for not having time for me. They only want my info if it's going to be big and easy. I do all the work for them." Brent replied, "I'm going to hold you to the part about calling me first. If I take my guys out there on a weed case, you better remember us on the next big one. I don't want to hear about you giving one to the local DEA boys, if I do, I'll never answer your calls again." "Hey Brent, you're the best. Don't worry, I won't forget you" said a grateful Johnny.

Brent hung up the phone and looked at the group. Only Val paid attention to the conversation. He was looking at Brent when he hung up the phone. Val said, "Don't tell me, Skinny Johnny?" "Yeah, he's got a weed case going. It sounds pretty easy. I'll probably look at it later tonight."

Mingo, not even looking up from the solitaire game said, "A weed case. Are you going to make me break away from all the stuff I've got going for a bunch of damned old weed?" Brent replied, "Yeah well, I can see you're awfully busy on a big case there. You don't have to go if you don't what to. You're pretty much worthless anyway." Mingo then said, "Oh, don't get all pissy. I'll break away from this case to help you. I'd hate to see you get killed out there because I wasn't there to protect you." Brent replied, "I appreciate that. What would I do without you?" Mingo loudly retorted, "Hell, I don't know. After all, I did teach you everything you know." To which Brent replied, "What are you talking about? I don't even know how to play solitaire."

Knowing there was a few hours to kill before the possibility of anything happening, Brent took care of his paperwork, while Val finished his crossword. The two men drove together to a sporting goods store. They were walking the aisles of the saltwater fishing tackle killing time when Val asked, "Hey, what's the story about Skinny Johnny? How did you start working with him?" Brent explained, "A guy I used to work with in homicide went to interview a murder suspect after he bonded out of jail. He said he didn't do the murder and he could prove it. He said he could tell the homicide guy who did. He also said he wanted to make a goodwill gesture by giving him a dope case. It was Johnny, who at the time, was a member of the, "Vato Locos" gang.

Val asked, "Oh, so your snitch was one of the crazy guys, huh?" Brent was teasing with Val and said, "Come on, Val. Don't call him a snitch. That word is degrading. You can call him a former gang member if you want to, but don't call him a snitch." To which Val said, "Oh okay, tell me how you started working with your former, gang member." Brent said, "Okay, that's better. He was mostly involved in the drug part of the gang. He never got popped for drugs, so I guess he was pretty good at it. Being charged with the murder caused him to see the light. He told my old homicide buddy he could give information about the gang's drug trafficking. The homicide guy put me in touch with Johnny. He's given me some pretty good cases. The DEA got wind of him and recruited him away from me.

Johnny went with the DEA because they pay better than us. I want to cut him off for not giving me the info he gives them, but when he calls, it's usually pretty good."

Brent then asked, "You know Val, the night I met you at the Cadillac, Rene told me something about you I've always wanted to ask about." "Ask away old buddy." replied Val. "Is it true you were the library club president at Memorial?" Val laughed a little and said, "Yeah, that's true. It's not really something I spread around. I'm not ashamed of it, but I do get teased about it." Brent asked, "Did the tuff guys at the school give you any trouble about it?" Val explained, "No, I didn't have any trouble at all. I think my classmates were a little mystified by me. They thought it was strange that someone would like to read. I don't think they knew what to make of it. I think it was sort of the way Native Americans wouldn't mess with lunatics. They probably figured I'd been touched by the gods, so they left me alone. I don't mean to brag, but I think it was my experience with the library club that made me such a good report writer."

Brent said, "I appreciate your help in that area. Your lessons have made me a better report writer."

Val said, "I guess I've taught you a couple of things, Brent. Let's see, I taught you how to write a good report. I taught you it's better to drink beer before a buy. And I said you should learn how to buy dope in Spanish. Now, that is some good information. You'll go far in this profession with that kind of help."

As Brent and Val looked at rods and reels, Brent's phone rang. Brent looked at Val and said, "Here we go."

Brent answered and heard, "Hey bro, I just dropped off the key to room 131. The guy is a Mexican. You know, like a Mexican from Mexico." Brent asked, "How do you know he's from Mexico?" The voice on the phone said, "I had a little trouble talking to him. I don't really speak Spanish. You know, it's Tex-Mex. This dude speaks real Spanish, like he's from down in Mexico."

Brent started getting excited about the news and asked, "Yeah, that is kind of interesting. Are they on the way to the motel?"

The informant then said, "I don't know, but you guys be careful. This dude seems like he's the real deal.

I mean if the info is true, he could be dangerous."

Brent hung up the phone and had a strange look on his face. He looked a Val and said, "Johnny said this guy's a Mexican." Val said, "Oh, now there's a shocker. A Mexican in south Texas. What are you talking about? You're the only white guy in our group."

Getting frustrated with Val, Brent said, "No asshole, I mean a guy from Mexico. Come to think of it, when Johnny called me earlier, he said the deal was supposed to be related to the Hernandez Cartel."

Val said, "That doesn't make any sense. Why would they be crossing the amount of weed that can fit in a motel room?" Brent replied, "That's exactly what I was wondering. Maybe we'll get lucky and find a kilo or two mixed in with the weed. Brent used his push to talk phone to say, "Mingo, Harry, Jimmy, get somewhere on the street side of the Rainbow. Me and Val will get in the parking lot close enough to see what's going on."

One by one, Mingo, Harry and Jimmy answered OK.

It was after eight o'clock in the evening and the sun was down. The parking lot was dimly lit by a few security lights. It was just dark enough to provide cover for the surveillance. Val positioned his car well away from the motel, but close enough to see the front of room 131. The view was good because it was a two story, one-wing motel.

Val asked Brent, "Do you know what kind of car we're looking for?"

Brent said, "No, Johnny didn't say, and I didn't think to ask. I doubt they would have let him see what type of car they were in anyway." Brent hit the push to talk again and said, "Mingo, get on the radio and see if you can get us a patrolman to help. Tell him to stay out of the area until we move in." "Ok." replied Mingo.

Things started happening quickly. As Brent and Val watched the front of room 131, a red pickup pulled up and parked. Brent told the group, "There's a red truck in front of the room. The doors are opening, and two guys are getting out. They're taking duffle bags out of the back seat of the truck and going into the room. Ok men let's roll on up there. Take your time, they aren't going anywhere."

The four undercover cars and one marked police vehicle drove up to the room. As they did, the two men walked out of the room and toward the truck. They were getting two more duffle bags out when they saw the officers. The two men saw the cars coming toward them and stood still on both sides of the truck. The men knew it was the police, but they didn't run. The detectives and the patrolman got out of their cars and walked toward the men. Brent walked up to the man standing on the driver's side of the truck and said, "We're the police. What's in those bags?"

The two men just stood still on both sides of the truck and said nothing. Brent and Val stood near the person on the driver's side. Mingo, Harry, Jimmy and the patrolman stood near the other. The man Brent and Val were standing next to seemed to be looking around assessing his options. Brent knew immediately that means trouble. Brent reached out to grab one of the man's arms. The man pulled away and reached for his waistband. Brent yelled, "Gun!", and the fight was on.

The detectives and the patrolman were trying to control men on both sides of the truck. Standing behind the man that reached for a gun, Brent put his right arm around his neck and lifted him off the ground. Brent figured if his feet were off the ground, he couldn't go anywhere. As he held the man up, Val furiously felt around the man's waistband searching for a gun. Val found a pistol and removed it from the man's waistband then he yelled, "I got a gun", to warn the men on the other side of the truck. Brent then slammed the man to the ground. That stunned the man into semi-consciousness. Val grabbed a pair of handcuffs from is back pocket and cuffed the man as he laid face down in the parking lot. Then Val turned his attention to the other side of the truck and asked," Are y'all all right over there?" Mingo answered, "Yeah, we're all right, but this guy's head has sprung a leak." Breathing heavily, Val said, "Damn, I didn't think guys hauling weed would be carrying guns."

The five officers drug the two suspects and the other two duffel bags into the open motel room. Now in the lighted room, the officers could get an idea of how much weed they recovered. While opening one of the large bags, "Mingo said, "It's quite a bit of weed, Brent." Each bag contained about thirty plastic wrapped, duct taped bundles. While placing one of the bundles on the bathroom counter, Mingo said, "Man, they sure must have bundled this weed good, I can't even smell it." Mingo took a pocket knife out of his pants pocket and cut open one of the bags. While his back was turned to the others, Mingo groaned and said, "Oh shit Brent, it's not weed." "Confused and worried, Brent asked loudly, "What do you mean it's not weed. What the hell is it?" Surprised by what Mingo said, all in the room were looking toward him. Mingo turned around to face them and had bundles of money in both hands. He said, "It's cash!"

Their stunned silence filled the room for a few seconds as they turned to stare at each other. Brent looked at one of the men in custody and asked, "Is it all money?" The suspect didn't speak, he just stared at Brent with a look of contempt on his face. Only Mingo and Val had ever seen this much money before. Brent looked at the duffle bags and guessed, "There's got to be hundreds of thousands of dollars." Val looked at the bags and said, "I think it could be a million if there's C-notes in there."

Brent saw one of the suspects staring out through the open door. That reminded Brent of the four-door sedan he and Val saw in the parking lot with the two men. It caused him to look at Val and ask, "What about those two guys out there?" Val looked at the patrol officer and said, "Why don't you and I go out there and check on them." Harry said, I'll go with him, Val. You've got plenty of work to do in here." Harry and the patrolman walked out of the room. They looked across the parking lot and saw the car was still there. There was enough light to see the car and see the men were no longer in it.

Harry told Val, "Why don't you stay here with the money and the crooks. I'd hate to leave Brent and Mingo alone. They are still in shock from seeing that much money." Harry looked at the officer and said, "I can see the car, but it looks like the guys are gone. Let's go check it out. We can get the plate and maybe we can figure out who it belongs to."

Harry and the patrolman walked up to the car and saw the windows down. When they saw the windows down, they stopped and looked at each other. They wondered why anyone would leave a car parked and not roll up the windows. Just then, one man popped up from behind the steering wheel, and the other from the back seat.

The quiet parking lot erupted in deafening noise. Bright muzzle flashes and the sound of automatic gunfire filled the parking lot. The two men fired more than one hundred rounds in a few seconds. Harry and the patrolman were shot to pieces. They were hit so many times, and so quickly, they didn't have time to move. They were killed instantly. The bullets that didn't hit them caused car windows to explode, and all the cars in the general area were riddled with bullet holes.

Val watched in horror as one of his best friends and the patrol officer were killed before his eyes. Val screamed, "Harry!", pulled his pistol and ran toward the gunfire. Brent, Jimmy and Mingo ran out of the room with guns in hand, just in time to see the car speeding out of the parking lot and down the road.

Val and Mingo ran toward the two crumpled, bloody bodies lying in the parking lot. Brent started running too but worried the two prisoners could still be a threat.

Jimmy and Mingo stood over the two bodies as Val sat on the ground and held Harrys' head in his arms.

Val cried over and over, "Harry, oh Harry!"

Chapter 8 Goodbye Harry

This wasn't the first time a member of the SAPD Narcotics office was killed in the line of duty. It's a dangerous job. There are undercover transactions that often lead to the UC officer being robbed for the buy money. The crooks that do the robbery think they're just robbing another junkie. They don't have any moral issues with holding a gun on someone and taking their money, they are after all criminals. The detectives are often executing, High Risk, warrants. More times than not, methamphetamine users suffer from paranoia. During the execution of a warrant, the meth addicts are convinced everyone is out to get them and the best response is violence. All these scenarios and more, require a large amount of planning and the best understanding of the suspect they can achieve. Given the amount of exhaustive effort put into the planning of an operation, you can't ensure no one will be injured or killed. The danger always exists, as mentioned above, it is a dangerous job.

Harry was killed on a hot steamy night at eight-thirty on August 7th, 1996. He was buried the following Saturday. Jimmy was the only one of the work group that didn't make the funeral. He buried his mother the month before after a long struggle with Alzheimer's. His dad died a month before that. During her illness, Jimmy had to take care of his mom the best he could. Her needs increased to the point he had to put her in a nursing home. He visited her every day until she passed. He didn't have the emotional strength to go to the funeral of his close friend.

After carrying Harry to his resting place, Brent, Mingo and Val stood over the grave long after the others were gone. They stood quietly with their own thoughts. Eventually Mingo said, "Well, how 'bout the Cadillac?"

It was only three and the bar didn't open until five, but they figured Jesse would let them in. They arrived to find the door locked and knocked loudly. Jesse ran to the door, unlocked it and welcomed them in. After the men entered, Jesse locked the door and turned to the men and shook each of their hands. Jesse spoke with a somber tone in his voice, "Gentlemen, I'm glad to see you." He walked them across the room to their usual table. Other than Jesse, one waiter and the kitchen staff, Mingo, Val and Brent were the only three in the bar. As they reached the table it was obvious there were five seats around it. Jimmy and Harry were not there.

The men sat down, and Jesse spoke, "Gentlemen, please accept my deepest condolences. Harry was a wonderful man. He was also a good friend. You probably don't know it, but he and I first met when we were young men and I was a dishwasher here. He gave me some good advice then. He was a good friend. Whatever you want is on the house. Allow me to make this small token of appreciation for Harry's friendship and for yours. It's the least I can do for you who must be in great pain. I'm sorry I wasn't at the funeral."

All three looked up at Jesse and Mingo spoke, "Thank you, Jesse. We will accept your kind offer and make a toast to Harry." Jesse snapped his fingers in the air and yelled, "Arthur", summoning his best waiter. Arthur arrived at the table with their beer. They didn't have to order, Arthur knew what beer to bring. He knew them well and brought them the same order a hundred times. Arthur said, "I'm sorry to hear about Harry. This table doesn't look quite the same without him here." Arthur placed the beers on the table and walked away. The three sat quietly at the table for a while when Val finally spoke. "Brent, I know what you're thinking. You think because you took us out to that motel, it's your fault. Just get that out of your mind once and for all. What happened out there that night was a bad accident. Anyone of us could have walked out to that car. You'll drive yourself crazy thinking you should have done something different. You wonder, what if I didn't answer Skinny Johnny? Or, what if I had blown him off like DEA did?"

Brent said, "I can't stop thinking about it. I haven't had any sleep since that night. If I'd made a different decision those two men would still be alive. I think about Harrys' children. I think about the patrolman's wife and kids. All I had to do was let it go and things would be different."

Val interjected, "You're right Brent, and the Hernandez Cartel would still have a million dollars to do business with. Now with a sterner voice Val said, "Ok, I've tried to put it to you nicely, but you're hard headed and naive. Let me put it to you this way. You're going to have to suck it up and go on. Before you got here, Mingo and I buried two of our friends. We mourn appropriately when this sort of thing happens and go back to work. The fact is this is a dangerous job. Bad things are going to happen occasionally. For all we knew Harry and the officer were approaching an empty car. There's no mistake in that, it's just bad luck. You just hope to get away with it most of the time. We usually do get away with it, and this time we didn't. If you'd screwed up, I would be the first to tell you so. It's just a fact, sometimes bad things are going to happen. This time it was as bad as it gets. That's all there is to it. If you can't get that through your thick skull maybe you'd be better off going back to homicide and handling misdemeanor cases. You wouldn't have to worry about someone getting hurt then."

Val knew how much Brent hated that kind of work. Brent was pissed off and didn't know quite how to take Val's lecture. Brent glared at Val without saying anything. He stared at Val as Val took another drink of his beer. Mingo sensed a bad situation was about to unfold and spoke up. "Brent, Val's not messing with you. Believe it or not, he's trying to help you get through it. Mingo looked at Val and then at Brent and said, "I probably would have said it a different way, but Val's pretty worked up and so are you. Don't forget, Val and Harry were very close. They came to the office at the same time. Reggie taught some UC stuff to Val and I taught some of the street stuff to Harry. I'll tell you another thing, we don't wonder if you're cut out for this kind of work. We know you are. You've proven you have what it takes. This is just your first experience burying one of your friends. Hopefully you'll never have to do it again, but you never know. I suggest we get our revenge by trying to figure out who did this and make them pay for it. Revenge is a great motivator. Let's use it."

The next Monday afternoon at two o'clock, Mingo Val, Brent and Jimmy were sitting quietly at their desks when Captain Terry Smith walked into the office area. He said hello to the four and then walked into Sgt. Clower's office. Mingo said, "Oh shit, here we go. We're about to find out what we did wrong and what we should do to make sure it never happens again. It probably comes from the chief and some of the other Monday morning quarterbacks. You don't hear from them if you're doing a great job. I don't think I've ever heard a speech after a good case. But they will surely let you know if something goes wrong. "

Brent heard Sgt. Clower yell from his office, "Brent, come here!"

Brent hung his head, got up from his desk and walked slowly toward the sergeants' office. Brent entered the office and saw his boss sitting behind his desk and Captain Smith sitting in one of the two chairs in front of the desk. Sergeant Clower told Brent, "Shut the door and have a seat." Captain Smith started the conversation, "The first thing I want you to do is relax. This isn't going to be an ass chewing. Although there are a lot of second guessers in the department, I don't think you could have done anything different the other night. When I got here as a detective, Harry was one of the first guys I rode with. I've been friends with the guys in your group for a long time. When I was promoted to sergeant, I always hoped to come back here, but the brass thought I was too close to the guys and too young to handle supervising them. When I made lieutenant, I couldn't get back here either. Now that I'm a captain I finally got transferred back. Of course, now I'm older and just a paper pusher not a narc. Val, Mingo and Harry trained me. I guess I'm trying to say I know what you're going through because I've been there. Unfortunately, this office has to go right back to work. I got a call today from the special agent in charge of the South Texas DEA office. He had a long-winded speech about how you guys stepped on one of their active cases. He said they were ready to go get that money and you guys got in their way. Brent, did you have any idea the DEA was working that case?" Brent tried to maintain his professionalism and stated, "No, and with all due respect captain, that long-winded speech he gave you was a bunch of bullshit. My informant told me he tried to give it to them, but they didn't want it. They told him they didn't have time to be bothered with a weed case. I guess they thought they were too good for that and would let the little old city boys do a weed case." Captain Smith continued, "Don't get me wrong, I'm not accusing you of anything. I believe you. It's not the first time I got a call from DEA saying, your guys have screwed up our case. We've been working that case for a long time and was just about to close it out. It seems that every big case we make is stepping on their toes. Did you know the motel case had something to with the Hernandez Cartel?" Brent replied, "The informant mentioned it could be, but I didn't believe him. He said it was supposed to be a couple hundred pounds of weed. I didn't know anything about money. In fact, that's why the DEA wouldn't talk to him about it, they thought it was a weed case." Captain Smith continued, "Well, don't misunderstand me, I believe you. I also want you to know you guys just made the largest seizure of money in the history of the office. If it hadn't been for the horrible misfortune of what happened to Harry and the patrolman, we would be in front of the local news TV cameras talking about it. To smooth over things with DEA, I've agreed to let them assign one of their guys to your group. We're going to work jointly to see if we can make the Hernandez Cartel pay for what they've done. The agent they're sending over is a good guy. His name is Ricky Terrell. Mingo and Val know him, he's been here before. They've worked together on cases including a few wiretaps. Ricky's got a degree in criminal justice from Alabama. But don't hold it against him, he's pretty much just a good ole boy. I think you'll like him. He probably thinks you might hold it against him the way DEA has said you stepped on their case. Give him a chance. The DEA has a lot of resources we don't. You guys can probably do some big things if you work together."

Brent said, "Well, if Val and Mingo like him I will too. Don't worry captain, I'll be a good host. Whatever help we can get is welcome. "

The Captain continued, "Brent, it sounds like you've got your mind right. We need to see how many of the Hernandez boys we can put in prison for the rest of their lives." Brent wanted to ask, but was somewhat unsure, "Ok, captain, did you have to fade any heat over this deal?" Laughing the captain said, "Oh yeah, the chief had a cow. But screw him, he has a couple of cows a day. Let's see if I can figure out the number of cows. Two cows a day, twelves years as the chief. Hell, he must have had enough cows to stock the King Ranch!"

Brent left the office with a singular focus...make the Hernandez Cartel pay for killing his good friend and the patrolman at that damn hotel. He was willing to work with whoever and wherever to make it happen, he didn't care if it was the DEA or the FBI or the Bexar County Sheriff's Department. He had only one thing on his mind...revenge.

Chapter 9 Ricky's Here

Monday afternoon was a little different for Brent than usual. First, he was running a little late, and when he entered the narcotics office there was someone there, he didn't know. There was a stranger talking with Jimmy, Val and Mingo. They were laughing and joking. Brent thought the man had a noticeable southern accent, but not like a Texas accent, more of a South Eastern United States accent.

When Brent entered the office, he walked toward his desk. Mingo, Val, Jimmy and the new guy stopped talking and turned to look at Brent. Val, still with a big smile on his face said, "Hey Brent, this is Ricky Terrell." Ricky walked toward Brent and put out his hand. The smile he wore earlier turned to a more professional, serious look. He and Brent shook hands very formally. Ricky said, "Brent, it's very nice to meet you. Val has told me a lot about you. I work for the DEA. I'm looking forward to working with you and the group. I worked with these boys a while back. It was probably just before you got here."

Val took control of the initial meeting and said, "Well, let's sit down and talk things over. Let's decide what we're going to do to make a big, DEA type case." The men sat around in the open office area. Ricky started the conversation, "Brent, I want you to know I'm not here to take your case. I just want to offer the DEA's help and make available the resources we have. I knew Harry, not well, but we worked on a couple of cases over the years. I want to offer whatever help I can to try to bring his, and the patrolman's killers to justice. I also think we can probably seize a lot of dope, properties and cash during the process.

Brent responded, "I appreciate that Ricky, but I've already had to explain my actions to my captain regarding what happened at the motel. Your boss called here and said we stepped on a DEA case by what we did at the motel. The captain and Val have told me you're a pretty good guy. But having to deal with that kind of bull shit is a bad way to start an investigation."

Mingo and Val cringed. They hoped the men could get through the initial meeting without the situation becoming contentious. Ricky didn't even flinch when he heard Brent's remark. The look on Ricky's face remained pleasant. Ricky smiled and said, "I don't blame you for being pissed off. You guys were at that motel doing the best you could, and bad things happened. The last thing you need is to get some bull shit from the DEA. I can understand the problems he's caused you because he has caused problems for me too. He and I have a working relationship, that's it. It doesn't surprise me he made a phone call like that to chew on the local law enforcement agency. I'd like to apologize for him as I've never heard him offer an apology to anyone, so I hope you will accept mine. I hope you don't hold a grudge against me for what he did, because I don't work like that."

Ricky's statement disarmed Brent. Brent thought about it for a minute and said, "Oh, there's no need for you to apologize. If you can tell me you're going to shoot straight with us and not hold any information back, we're all going to get along just fine." Ricky replied, "Brent, you have my word. Anything I know, you'll know. I wish I could promise that for the entire agency, but I can't. What I can promise is, I'm here to do whatever I can to help you guys. I was selected to come over here because Val and I've worked together before and we got a lot of good work done. I value my relationship with your office and wouldn't do anything to hurt that."

Brent said, "That all sounds good, but I did notice something about you that makes you different than us." Now cringing again, Val, Jimmy and Mingo waited to hear what Brent was going to say. Brent continued, "You sound like you're from LA." Ricky thought about that for a second and asked, "LA?"

Brent chuckled, "Yeah, lower Alabama."

All had a good laugh. Ricky said, "Yeah, my family lives on a little farm outside of Mobile and they won't talk to me anymore. They say I'm not really from the Terrell clan because I have a college degree and all my teeth. They made me leave home. Now, there's only nine of them in a one room shotgun shack with a leaky roof."

Val said, "Brent, Ricky was telling us they believe they can get up on a wire by the end of the week. The DEA has targets on both sides of the border. Some are in the San Antonio area. They know these guys are crossing loads of dope going north, and money going back south." Ricky chimed in, "Yeah, the cartel owns a large trucking company. We're pretty sure they're running the dope North concealed under loads of produce. It's cheap to use produce as a cover load. Boy, what a pain in the ass to unload or search the trailer full of vegetables or fruit. Most of our guys would rather cut their finger off than move a trailer into a parking lot, find a forklift, and unload fifty thousand pounds of watermelons. All that work is done taking a chance you might find a load of dope in the front of the trailer. There's also a chance the load of produce will be damaged during the process. If you find dope, it's no big deal. You can do whatever you want to with the produce. But, if you don't find dope, there will always be an "alleged", owner of the produce submitting a hundred thousand dollars claim for damaged produce. Unless you've got some very reliable info, the load of dope is going to make it to Dallas, Atlanta, or somewhere further north. Although we have a pretty good idea how the dope is coming in, were not sure how the money is going back south. Our guess is it's probably going back in empty trailers. We haven't found a trailer loaded with money. They could be taking the trailer apart and concealing the money in the frame, the walls of the trailer, who knows, then put it back together. Tearing apart a trailer looking for something you're not sure is there is really taking a chance on a lawsuit."

Val said, "Brent, the DEA wants me to be the monitor of the wire since it's likely ninety five percent of the calls will be in Spanish. You, Mingo and Jimmy will be mobile with a few other agents. If we get a tip on a load, you guys can contact patrol and make traffic stops on the target vehicles." Ricky complemented Val saying, "I think Val is responsible for some of the biggest cases our office has ever made. He's legendary at being able to pick things out of a phone call other people never hear and he can document the calls better than the civilians. It's a shame he has to fix most of the other written translations."

With a big smile on his face Ricky turned to Val and said, "Hey Val, do you remember those roosters you seized on the last wire?" Val replied, "Yeah, I remember. But that wasn't my fault.

Don't say I seized any roosters. I didn't have anything to do with it." Ricky went on to explain, "Our group supervisor had Val monitoring the calls originating in Mexico on the last wire. It's important the monitor be able to speak Spanish, but it's more important the monitor be able to identify the coded language in the calls. You will never hear the trafficker say, I'll be sending a hundred kilos of cocaine on a tractor-trailer hidden in a load of lettuce. The code for the narcotics lingo is only limited by the imagination. It's the monitor's responsibility to try to figure out the code. In the past, the kilos have been referred to as batteries, watermelons, oranges, tires you name it. When Val and I worked the last wire, Val told me about how it was important to listen to how things were being said, as much as what is being said."

Val said, "Yeah, it's true. It's important to listen hard to every call. You might hear a guy say the same words hundreds of times and they it doesn't mean anything. Then you'll hear the same words being said, but it's said with more seriousness or urgency. I don't really know how to explain it, but when I hear it, I just know it means something different. When Ricky mentioned roosters, he's talking about the rooster case. One day I heard one of the guys talk about roosters on a call. I just wrote it down like it was said. It didn't mean anything to me. The calls were coming in much faster than I could do the transcription, so I was just taking notes. All the calls are digitally recorded, dated and time stamped as they come in. Even if they're coming fast, I can always go back to the recording and take my time with the transcription. Ricky's boss, Doug Garland came into the room and saw my notes. He read the line about roosters and asked me how many calls I was behind. I told him I don't know, a hundred, maybe a hundred and ten.

There were a lot of calls waiting for me to listen to and write down. It was early in the investigation and I didn't have a good sense of the code the traffickers were using. There hadn't been any interdiction efforts yet. Sometimes, I would have to guess about what they were saying and pass the guess along to the guys itching to make a stop. Depending on what was found on the traffic stop, it might let me know if I'm on the right track. If dope or money was found on the stop, a piece of the puzzle would come together. It's a little easier when you start understanding the codes."

Val continued, "One night I was working with the lead investigator and Doug walked into the wire room. He wanted to read some of the transcripts. One of them caught Doug's eye. He got all excited when he read about 20 roosters being transported from San Antonio to Houston in a Cadillac. Doug smarted off," Hay Val, why didn't you tell us about this call?" I told him, well I'm not sure there's anything to it. He got kind of pissy and asked, don't you think it's odd that "roosters", are being driven from San Antonio to Houston in a Cadillac? I said yeah, I agree it sounds a little odd, I mean, I've never seen a Cadillac going down the road full of roosters. But I've heard some of the crooks talking about fighting roosters. They talk about fighting them in Mexico and in the states. I just figured it was fighting roosters they were talking about. Doug made a face and said, "I think we need to go out on this one." Val stated, "It didn't matter to me, I wasn't going to have to go out and find a Cadillac in the dark on IH 10 E. I didn't take it personally, I had plenty of work to do without worrying about that. I just went back to working on the calls. I didn't want to make him mad. I was working sixteen hours a day for the past two weeks. I was doubling my pay in overtime!"

Ricky said, "Doug called out all the guys assigned to the roadwork and had us on IH 10 looking for a Cadillac. I came across several Cadillacs on the road. It was like trying to find a needle in a haystack. I figured if we saw a Cadillac with a man and woman in the front seat, and three kids in the back, that's probably not the right one. Ninety percent of the Cadillacs on the road can be eliminated by sizing up the occupants. If our brother agency, Homeland Security, wasn't so politically correct and focused more on what terrorists normally look like, they would be more effective. No need to pull old women and children out of a line and search them in an airport. I mean, when was the last time an eighty-year-old woman set off a bomb?"

Ricky continued with the story, "Just east of Columbus I saw a white Cadillac with Mexican plates. I could see the tops of containers in the backseat, but I couldn't tell what kind of containers they were. I got on the radio and asked one of the guys in the wire room to call the Columbus PD and see if they could help us with a traffic stop. We were in luck, a marked unit was working radar just ahead of us.

Val said, "Man, there was a lot of excitement in the wire room. Doug and another agent high fived each other about making a traffic stop. They just knew they were going to put a good case on the table. They wanted to show the Assistant U.S. Attorney the case was working. I wasn't really caught up in the enthusiasm. I was still trying to get caught up on the calls. Doug looked at me with that, I told you so kind of face."

Ricky said," About the time the Columbus officer lit up his lights, two or three of the agents were catching up. The officer got the Cadillac stopped. It pulled to the shoulder of the road. We drove up and boy were we excited. We just knew we were going to make a big dope case or recover a bunch of money. We were just about to prove the justification for the wire. The Columbus officer, me and two other agents walked up to the car and got on both sides of the Cadillac. When we looked in the car, we saw ten small cages containing various types of fighting roosters in the backseat. We were starting to lose enthusiasm. Then we open the trunk and found ten more cages of roosters. "

Ricky continued, "I cracked up! I was bent over laughing and almost wet my pants. I looked up and saw the other two agents staring at me with angry looks on their faces. I had to tone it down a bit when I saw the other agents didn't think it was as funny as I did."

The guys listening to the story were laughing out loud. Val went on to explain what was going on in the wire room. "Doug was still hopping around like he won the lottery. He got on the radio and asked the agents what they found. I heard Ricky come on the radio and say," Uh, I'll give you a call." After hearing that, I kind of perked up and started watching Doug. I figured it wasn't good news. I've heard that kind of thing before. If it was good news, they would have put it out over the radio for everyone to hear. I watched as Doug answered the phone. He had his back turned to me. Doug listened to Ricky for about a minute, then hung up the phone. He didn't say a word, hell he didn't even look back at me. I could see the DEA group supervisors' face turn red."

Brent asked, "Are you telling me he didn't say you were right?"

Val explained, "No, he just walked out of the wire room all red faced. I had to guess they may have actually found roosters!"

Mingo said, "Oh man, before he left the room, I think I would've said I told you so."

Val replied, "Oh, I thought about it, but I was making a fortune in overtime. I was afraid he might relieve me."

Ricky said, "Yes sir boys, I'm proud to say I was on the case and contributed to the Great Rooster Caper. The rooster case is almost as famous as the screwup way the FBI caught Richard Jewell in that Olympic bombing case. Every time I hear an FBI agent bragging about how smart they are, I think about Richard Jewell. Y'all remember him, don't you? He was working a security gig in Atlanta during the Olympics. He tried to help and ended up being the prime suspect in the bombing. Poor guy, his picture was on every newscast and newspaper. He was eventually cleared but not before he was run through the ringer. When I hear an agent brag about something I ask, Hey, is that how y'all caught Richard Jewell? Gets them every time."

Chapter 10 The Wire is Up

Ten days after Ricky started working with the SAPD Narcotics group, the DEA submitted information to a federal judge for a Title III, a wiretap. The affidavit requested the monitoring of five phones of known members of the Hernandez Cartel. The federal judge granted permission to monitor the phones and make communication intercepts for ninety days.
The investigation was named, "The H Operation."

Val oversaw the wire room and the calls were coming in much faster than he could keep up. Val was assisted by two civilians during the day, but he was the only monitor in the wire room at night.

Mingo, Brent and Jimmy would be on the road ready to respond to any information where interdiction was warranted. The group was on the road with three other DEA agents assigned to the mobile surveillance. When the wire room received calls about suspect vehicles, the mobile units would make the stops.

At two o'clock on the first day of the wire, Ricky and Brent were at the office. Ricky asked Brent, "How about going for a ride. There's a restaurant we think was bought with dope money, you want to go see it?" Brent replied, "Yeah that sounds good, let's go."

They got in Ricky's car in the office parking lot. Ricky started the car then looked at Brent and asked, "Well son, are you ready to do some good?" Being excited to get the show on the road, Brent replied, "You better know it. I've been chomping at the bit waiting for this day. I can't wait to make some traffic stops. This is my first wire case authorized by a federal judge. There are a few things I was wondering. Can you go through a little question and answer session?"

Ricky said, "Well, I've worked six wires. I worked with Val on two. Ask me anything and I'll try to answer it. If I don't have the answer, I'll find it. What do you want to know?" Brent asked, "Well, for starters I almost fainted when I heard we could get all the overtime we wanted during the wire. I asked Mingo about that. He told me the feds would be paying the overtime. It didn't make much sense to me. Is it true the feds will pay for the overtime?"

Ricky explained, "Yes, that's true. But for the federal government to pick up the tab on overtime, a representative from the DEA has to present the case to an Assistant United States Attorney. Concerning this case, I made the initial presentation to the AUSA. I had to meet with her and explain why I believe the case would make an impact on an international drug trafficking, or money-laundering organization. In this case, the Hernandez Cartel does both. They are also involved in human trafficking. I don't know any specifics on that. The border patrol and customs work those kinds of cases. I've only heard some of the customs guys talk about it. The stories are horrible. They've told me about the cartel putting people in the trailers with the produce. Most of the produce trailers aren't air conditioned. Some of the people in the trailers die of heat stroke. The cartel charges four thousand per person and sometimes, the poor people don't get any help at all. Imagine that, a cartel lies to people and takes their money. I do know more about drug trafficking and money laundering. They import the drugs and try to legitimize the money made from sales. One of the ways they launder money is to buy businesses, just like the restaurant I'm about to show you. A restaurant is a good example. It doesn't matter whether the restaurant is successful or not. The cartel is always going to make it look successful. When the crooks go to the bank with the alleged profits of the restaurant, it looks like the money was made legally. If the AUSA's office agrees the case is worthy of federal funds, they classified it as an OCADETF case. The initials stand for Organized Crime and Drug Enforcement Task Force. After the case is classified as an OCADTF case, the Office of the National Drug Control Policy will provide funds to support the case."

Brent said, "Now I understand why the city said we could get as much overtime as we need. It's not costing them anything." Ricky replied, "You got it, Brent. It's set up that way so departments with limited funds can participate without having to worry about the money when the feds are paying the overtime. It also gets some officers motivated to work extra hours to pad their income. It's usually a win-win situation."

Brent asked, "I know the Hernandez Cartel traffics dope, but I don't know much about the organization. You got any history on that?" Ricky responded, "Yes sir, I do. Daniel Raymundo Hernandez is known as number three. He's the third person in the history of the organization to be in the top spot. His grandfather was the first. He's the one that organized the group in the early seventies. Back then, they were only running dope for the Colombians, they didn't own it. The old man died a natural death in 1989. It's pretty rare for a cartel leader to die of natural causes. He's probably the only one I've ever heard of to have that kind of luck. In the early eighties, they started buying coke from the Colombians and distributing it themselves. Profits shot up when they started selling their own dope. The Hernandez Cartel had the only game in town for about ten years. Some of the guys who were working for the Hernandez' thought it would be a good idea to start their own gang, and they did. The gangs coexisted for a while, but greed got the best of them. One of the gangs killed one of the old man's brothers when he took over after number one died. The old man's other brother really should have been in charge after the assassination, but he didn't have the stomach for it. The word is he ran to Belize with a pile of money. That created a void and there was a power struggle for about a year. Daniel Raymundo managed to come out on top of the struggle between he and several other members who thought they should be the boss. Danny Ray proved he was smarter and more ruthless than the others. If someone tried to rise up, he would have the guys family picked up, then tortured and killed right before his eyes. Then they would torture him to death. Danny Ray would take the rivals body and hang it off a bridge for all the others to see. He usually hangs a sign on them that says, this is what happens when you cross the cartel. It's a fairly effective management technique, don't you think, Brent?"

Brent then asked, "Danny Ray has been on a pretty good run. How does he manage to stay on top of the hill? Even Al Capone got arrested eventually." Ricky said, "They say he's got a pretty good system going. His whole life is like a shell game. He has several body doubles and ninety percent of the time, no one knows where he, or the doubles are. The doubles aren't to fool the Mexican and US governments. They are just there to fool the people that are closest to him. There are only a few people in the world that speak to him in person. The families of the people that can speak to him live in luxury in Mexico at Hernandez' expense. He doesn't pay for it because he's just a good old boy, it's because he wants the people around him to know, not only are their lives in his hands, but their family's lives are too." Ricky continued, "I've heard a story that one of his boys brought a cell phone into Daniel's house one time, and while he was there, his telephone rang. Hernandez' security men took the phone out of his pocket and smashed it. They made him apologize to Danny Ray for breaking the rules. He was then led outside, and they put a bullet in the back of his head. Danny Ray is careful about anything that could be a tracking device, or a recorder, or anything photographic. The only known picture of him was taken when he was nineteen and booked for a murder in Guadalajara. He sat in jail for about a month waiting for trial. While he sat in jail, all the witnesses to the murder were killed and Daniel was released. They couldn't go forward without a witness. He disappeared after that. About two weeks after he was released, the little police station where he was held burned down. The photograph of him and all the booking information was lost in the fire. We do have a set of prints from the murder arrest though. When he was booked for the murder, duplicate print cards were made. When the print man saw a card was already on file, he threw the second one in the trash. After the police station burned down, the Federales were looking through the trash trying to find any evidence related to the arson. They didn't find any evidence to the arson, but they did find the discarded print card. If it wasn't for that, there would be nothing in the world to identify him with. The DEA has heard a few times he comes in to San Antonio to shop at Easter with the rest of the tourists from Mexico. But, with no photo or any other current information, he could be sitting in this car with us and we'd never know it."

Brent asked, "Is there any speculation on how he crosses the border to go shopping?"

Ricky said, "No, nobody knows. He may be smuggled in the same way his dope is. They might smuggle him in hidden in one of the produce trailers. Maybe he's disguised as a big head of lettuce. I doubt he's coming to the United States on a commercial airliner in first class using his passport. He could be coming in on one of his private jets, or on one of his tour buses. The cartel has travel agencies and transportation companies on both sides of the border. We once got information he was sending tour buses full of people to Las Vegas to make payoffs with casino money."

Brent asked, "Casino money, how does that work?"

Ricky smiled and explained, "It's a pretty cool way to launder money and pay someone on this side of the border. Let's say he needs a member to pay someone involved in transportation in the United States. The member walks into a casino with a hundred thousand dollars. He goes to the counter and buys a hundred thousand in chips. He meets with the guy that needs to be paid and they play blackjack for a while. The member gives the chips to the other guy and they part ways. The transportation guy turns the chips in and gets ninety-nine thousand in cash. He's now paid off and while traveling home he has a good excuse for why he has a hundred thousand dollars cash in possession. He has documentation he was given for tax purposes at the casino. When he gets home with his money, he can deposit it or do whatever he wants with it. The money has been legitimized. It's pretty easy if you think about it. Say, you have a busload of gang members going to Las Vegas, you can take care of a lot of business and launder a lot of money in just a few days. Everybody leaves Las Vegas happy. The payoffs are made, and the gangsters have a good time. The traffickers on the US side are paid and the money is washed. What's not to love about that?"

Brent said, "I've got a lot to learn about the international side of trafficking and money laundering."

Ricky said, "Maybe so, but don't think for a minute we could do this kind of work without assistance from local departments. For one thing, we wouldn't get much done without the ability to make traffic stops. Remember something, the DEA is full of agents, not policemen. Most of them haven't been on the streets making calls or stops. Policeman have more knowledge about street activity and handling people than most agents do. You, Mingo, Jimmy and Val, have a lot to offer. I know we're going to be a good team working this case. I've got a good feeling about it."

Brent replied, "I sure hope so, Ricky. No case is ever going to bring Harry back, but it would help the way I feel about things. I'd like to make some of the Hernandez Cartel pay for what they've done." Ricky said, "Let me tell you something Brent, if I have anything to say about it, we'll make them pay."

By that time, Ricky drove his car into the parking lot of the gas station directly across the street from a very nice restaurant called Maggie's. Ricky looked at the restaurant then Brent and asked, "Are you familiar with Maggie's?"

"Yeah, I was in there lots of times when it was open." Brent replied.

With Brent's response, Ricky then asked, "What's wrong with you son, can't you see it's still open? How can you not see the thriving business going on there?"

Brent didn't understand what the heck Ricky was saying and asked, "What are you talking about, Ricky? It's been closed for months. How can you have a thriving business when the windows and doors are boarded up?"

Ricky explained, "The Hernandez Cartel bought it about two years ago. They've been laundering money through it ever sense. Their business records make it look like the restaurant is doing very well. In fact, they're showing one hundred ninety-five thousand in food and liquor sales every month. I guess they cap the money laundering at one ninety-five because they don't want to make it too obvious. With the money being laundered through the restaurant, they're buying houses and property in San Antonio." Brent said "Wow, I wish I had a boarded-up restaurant building that was bringing in one hundred ninety-five thousand a month. I never knew closed restaurants could be so profitable." Ricky then explained, "Brent, if things go right, our office and your office will own that restaurant by the end of this case. It's best if we get all the evidence, we need to close the case quickly. The longer businesses stay open and are operated with laundered money, the harder it is to make the case for seizure. The longer a business like that operates, the more it looks legitimate."

Chapter 11 Stopping the Truck

Val was in the wire room about two weeks monitoring calls between targets in Mexico and in San Antonio, Dallas and Atlanta. Day in, day out, he heard a lot of talk, but nothing he really considered important. Early on Friday night he heard one of the targets say, "We are going to cross the green in Laredo on Monday morning at eight." He called DEA group supervisor, Doug Garland, and told him he thought he had some decent information. Doug was excited about having their first useful piece of information from the wire. Doug said, "I'll be right there."

Doug walked in the wire room around thirty minutes later, pulled up a chair and sat next to Val. Doug said, "Val, I almost ran out of my house without my shoes when you called. I figured you wouldn't be calling unless you had something good. So, tell me all about it."

Val said, "I think we might have something. One of the guys in Mexico called another in Dallas. They spent some time talking about the trucking company. Most of the conversation was about some of the tractors. The conversation seemed to be strictly business. I mean, they were using vehicle numbers and license plates when talking about specific trucks. Then, toward the end of the conversation the guy in Mexico said, we're going to cross the green on Monday at eight."

Doug said, "That is pretty interesting. They spent some time on the phone call talking about trucks. Is it possible they could've been talking about a green truck? Or maybe a load of lettuce? I know you're a good judge of the conversations, Val. I'm just throwing it out there for conversation sake. If were looking for something crossing the border, were going to have to get a lot of people involved. We'll need to talk to customs, border patrol and send our mobile guys down there. I guess I just want to know if you feel strongly about them crossing something."

Val replied, "Yeah, I understand your concern Doug, but the tone of the conversation changed when the guy in Mexico mentioned the green. And the guy in Dallas sounded a little different too. They also mentioned running the green to Dallas. IH 35 runs from Laredo to Dallas, so that puts the whole trip on one side of the highway. If we can figure out something about the truck and trailer, we'll have hundreds of miles to spot it on IH 35. We'll have a lot of better chances than looking for something that's going to make four or five different changes in their route."

Doug was thinking aloud and said, "If they are going to cross the border in Laredo at eight, they'll be on IH 35 for two and a half hours from Laredo to San Antonio. If we do spot one of their trailers crossing at eight, we can just watch it until it gets here. Then the mobile guys can pull it over and do an inspection. It really won't be difficult to determine which one of the trailers it is along the highway, all the produce trailers have a big avocado, head of lettuce and watermelon painted on the side. If one of those cross at eight, we'll stop it in San Antonio and see what they're hauling."

Val asked, "You want me to call our guys and get them ready?"

Doug replied, "Yeah, we better be set up down south around seven. We'll have a couple of hours leeway between here and there. You call your guys and I'll call ours. We can get them staggered out on IH 35 starting at about Pearsall. We'll get a car positioned about every 20 miles. If one of the Hernandez trailers is crossing about eight, it should be easy to spot it coming north. I'll give Bobby Love a call. He can talk to the customs guys at Laredo and have them be on the lookout. If the customs guys spot it crossing, they can give us a heads up on the highway. Val asked, "Bobby Love, who the hell is Bobby Love?"

Doug explained, "He's a customs guy I've known for a long time. He's worked for customs for about thirty years. He won't be willing to get out on the road with us, but I can probably talk him into making a phone call."

Val leaned back in his chair, crossed his arms over his chest and said, "All right, I'm excited about something happening, but I'm not as excited as the guys on the road will be. Maybe we can get them out of the theatre and off the golf course. They have a target to watch for and it shouldn't be hard to spot a trailer with giant veggies and fruit painted on the sides."

On Monday morning at seven o'clock, the guys working the highway were in position. Three DEA agents and three SAPD officers would be on IH 35 looking for a Hernandez tractor-trailer.

Not long after the mobile guys were in position, Doug's phone rang. Doug answered and heard, "Hey bro, it's Bobby." "Well if it ain't Bobby Love, what's going on brother?" Bobby said, "I've got some good news for you. Your trailer just crossed at Laredo. I had to threaten to shoot some customs agents to keep them from jacking it up as it crossed. They figured if you are interested in the trailer, they should be too."

Doug said, "Oh Bobby, that wouldn't be cool. I'd hate to think your customs boys would steal one of my cases." Bobby stated, "I wouldn't steal one, but then again, I'm lazy and wouldn't make a case if it fell in my lap. But some of these young bucks are chomping at the bit to make their first big case. You know what I mean, it might get them a step increase or get them promoted if it's big enough. If it's a really big one, they might end up being a Group Supervisor like you." "You're the best Bobby, I don't care what the customs guys say about you!" said Doug. Laughing, Bobby said, "That makes two of us, I don't care either. I quit worrying about that sort of thing twenty-five years ago."

Doug ended his phone call with Bobby, then looked at Val and said, "It's on the way. I love it when you make me look so smart, Val. You might end up making me the regional boss." Doug gathered up some paperwork from the wire room. He went to a large file cabinet in the corner of the office. He took a key out of his pants pocket and unlocked the top drawer. He took a large envelope out of the drawer and said, "I'm going out there with the guys. I'd like to see what happens on this traffic stop."

Val said, "Good luck, Doug. I'll keep my fingers crossed."

About an hour and a half south of San Antonio, Mingo got on the radio and said, "I got the trailer on 35 south of Pearsall." Anticipating the tractor-trailer would stay on IH 35 and drive north through San Antonio, Ricky got on the radio and asked, "Can one of you PD guys arrange for a traffic stop on the south side of town?" Brent answered, "Yeah, I'll get on it. I'll ask one of the traffic guys to make it look like a DOT stop." Doug said, "That would be great, Brent, the uniformed officer can play it off as an inspection. Let the officer know about ten minutes after the stop Ricky and I will go to the truck."

As the Hernandez trailer traveled north on IH 35, three agents and three officers followed. Just south of San Antonio, the traffic officers fell in behind the produce trailer. The marked units initiated a traffic stop. The tractor-trailer pulled into a Walmart parking lot. After about five minutes. Ricky and Doug walked up and contacted the officers. They were wearing yellow windbreakers with large bold DEA letters on their back. Mingo, Brent and Jimmy watched from a distance while Ricky and Doug talked to the driver of the Hernandez truck.

Brent saw Mingo parked in the Walmart parking lot. He drove up to Mingo's car, got out and walked up to Mingo and said, "Man, this is exciting. I can't wait to see what's in the trailer." Mingo said, "Yeah, I'm glad you're here too. If there's a load of watermelons in the trailer, we're going to need somebody to unload them. I think that somebody is you. I'd like to help you, but my back has been bothering me lately."

Brent became agitated, "You, lazy bastard. Your back is always bothering you when you're trying to get out of work. Your back pain is probably caused from sitting at your desk all day playing solitaire." Mingo replied, "Hey, do you think I like having a bad back. You make it sound like I'm trying to get out of climbing up in a hot trailer and unloading watermelons by hand for three or four hours in ninety-five-degree heat."

As Mingo and Brent watched the activity of the traffic stop, they saw Doug and Ricky walk to the back of the trailer. Mingo said, "Here we go. Get ready to heft some watermelons, son?" While at the back of the trailer, only Ricky could see what Doug was doing. Doug got up under the back of the trailer and reached into the pocket of his yellow jacket. He pulled out the envelope he removed from the file cabinet. He took a small magnetic tracking device out of the envelope and placed it on the trailer in an area where it wouldn't be found.

Ricky saw all of Doug's movements. Just after Doug attached the tracker, Ricky asked, "Doug, what are you doing?" Doug explained, "Ricky, there's been little change of plans. We're going to let this one go. We'll track it north then stop it on the way back. I figure on the way back south, it will be loaded with money."

Ricky was livid, "Doug, the PD guys are out here expecting to knock off a load. What am I going to tell them about finding the trailer and then seeing nothing done? I'm sure they're expecting to see this trailer unloaded." Doug then stated, "You're going to tell them this was the wrong trailer. Tell them it's not the one we were looking for and we let it go after apologizing to the driver."

Ricky then said, "Hey Doug, I don't mean to be disrespectful, but this is a bunch of bullshit. I'm not going to lie to the guys who lost one of their friends and got this case started." Doug then told Ricky, "Well, you say whatever you want to. But if you tell them the truth, it will go bad for you, Ricky. There's always need for another agent in Iraq. They grow a lot of poppy fields down there. They also make a lot of heroin. You seem like a guy that could put a dent in that operation. You would probably only be there a year, maybe eighteen months. Don't you have a new baby? She's about two years old now, isn't she? By the time you get back home, she won't even know who you are. Now Ricky, you should see it my way. I hate to think you're going to talk your PD buddies about this. Let me know if you'd like to see Afghanistan. Maybe you'd like that better than Iraq. I can put in the transfer for a new agent tomorrow."

Ricky stood and looked at Doug in amazement and disgust. He knew he was stuck between a rock and a hard place.

Doug walked up to one of the patrol officers conducting a traffic stop and inspection. He told him, "When you're done with the inspection, just let it go."

As Mingo, Brent and Jimmy watched from a distance, the truck slowly pulled back on to IH 35 and continued north. Brent asked Mingo, "What the hell is going on here? Aren't we going to search the trailer?" Mingo replied, "I don't know. I thought that's why we were out here. Are they going to just let it roll?" Mingo got on the radio and asked, "Hey Ricky, was going on? Aren't we going to search it?"

Ricky was still standing on the side of the road next to Doug as the Hernandez truck and trailer headed north. He didn't know what to tell them, especially over a radio. Ricky thought, what am I going to tell these guys? When this thing started, I gave them my word I wouldn't hold anything back. After considering it for a few seconds, Ricky got on his radio and said, "Uh, I'll give you guys a call in a little bit and let you know. I guess we're done for today."

Doug glared at Ricky then got on his radio and said, "Okay guys, were done for today. That wasn't the right trailer, but thanks for the help."

Val was in the wire room listening to the radio transmissions and was as confused as anyone else. Val said, "What does he mean the wrong trailer? It crossed at eight and we know it belongs to the cartel. How could it be the wrong trailer? Val picked up his phone and called Ricky. Ricky answered the call with apprehension. "Hello." Val was livid, "Ricky, what's going on out there? How can it not be the right trailer?" Ricky replied, "Well, Doug checked it out and said there was nothing to it." Val continued with his questioning, "Nothing to it? It crossed at the right time. It belongs to the right company, and it was on the

right route. How can there be nothing to it?" Ricky wanting to diffuse the situation said, "I don't know Val, why don't you call your guys and we'll meet tonight. I'll try to explain when it's just the five of us." Val was still incensed, "Ricky, I'm up here busting my ass to stay on top of these calls. I get you a good target and you let it go?" Still very much on the defensive, Ricky said, "Val, I don't have anything for you right now. It wasn't my decision. When you shut down the wire room tonight, give Mingo, Brent and Jimmy a call and we'll meet for a few beers." Val implored, "Okay Ricky, but don't stand us up on this one. You might have a mutiny on your hands." Ricky said, "Don't worry about it I'll be there. I might be a little scared, but I'll be there. Try to get the boys calmed down a little bit before I get there."
Val said, "I'll do what I can, but I can't guarantee anything."

That night Val, Mingo, Brent and Jimmy were sitting at their favorite table at Hills and Dales beer joint. Ricky wasn't there yet. Jimmy said, "I'm going to be pissed off if Ricky doesn't show up." Val said, "Oh, I think he'll be here. I know the DEA has treated us like borrowed mules in the past, but Ricky has never lied to me, I think he'll show up."

Trying to change the mood at the table a little, Val asked Brent, "Hey, did you hear about your old buddy at homicide, Rene?" Without interest or looking at Val, Brent said, "No, what about him?" Val said, "I heard he's going to retire in a few weeks, the day he hits twenty. He's going to take an assistant chief's job at the airport." Brent chuckled, "Well, isn't that something. One day he's a lowly homicide detective, and the next, he's an assistant chief at the airport. I guess all that kissin' ass did him some good after all. He told me it would. He's going to be an assistant chief, and I always thought he was going to be mayor." Jimmy laughed and said, "And the whole time you are making fun of him, he was lining up big things. Who's the dumb ass now, Brent?" Brent just shook his head staring at the floor, then he looked up and asked Val, "What did Ricky tell you on the phone?" "He said, Doug told him it wasn't the right trailer. That's why they decided to let it go." Brent was starting to get upset again and said, "Are you shittin' me? It all matched up. It was exactly what we were looking for." Val said, "I don't know. I said pretty much the same thing to Ricky."

Just then, Ricky walked in through the front door and glanced over at the table where the PD guys were sitting. As he walked up, he didn't get a warm welcome. All three just stared at him as he made his way to the table. Ricky thought, oh, this is not going to be good. Ricky hoped his southern charm would carry the day. He sat down and managed a big smile. Ricky asked, "What's goin' on boys?"

They were in no mood for small talk. Val said, "Well, let's hear it Ricky." Ricky took a deep breath and said, "Okay, Doug decided to let this one go, and stop it on the way back. Now, I'm shooting straight with you guys. Please keep it to yourselves, if that's possible. Doug threatened to send me back to the desert if I told you the truth. I was a loadmaster on a C-130 and flew over that damn sand for fourteen months. I don't want to go back. Val asked, "How are you going to know when it's coming back? Hell, it was hard enough to find when we knew where, and when it was going to cross." Ricky took a deep breath, sighed and said, "Uh, because it has a tracker on it."

The three detectives looked like they were ready to beat Ricky. Brent threw both hands up in the air and said, "Oh, so you put a tracker on it. Did you have this planned all along?" Ricky replied, "No, I thought we were out there to trying to knock off a load." Brent said, "Well, it was only you and Doug at the back of the trailer. Who had a tracker ready to go?" Ricky replied, "I wasn't lying to you when I told you, if I know it, you'll know it. Doug put the tracker on the trailer." Mingo said, "Oh, so Doug planned this all along." Ricky sighed again and said, "Maybe we should consider it a change of plans, rather than pulling a fast one." Jimmy said, "No one walks around every day with a tracker in their pocket. The plans must have changed before the stop was made. With that kind of change in game plans, why didn't we know about it?" Ricky explained, "Because, I didn't know about it." Jimmy asked, "Why didn't you know about it?" Ricky knew his audience was having a hard time believing what he was saying, he continued, "I don't know, I guess he had his reasons. I told you about my relationship with Doug. I'm sure there's lots of things he doesn't tell me. It's hard enough for me and him to have a civil conversation, much less him telling me something on his mind about how a case is headed."

Brent said, "Well, I think this is all a bunch of bullshit. What are you trying to tell us, you don't trust us? You trusted us enough for Val to identify a target. You trusted us enough for us to get out on the road and find the truck. You trusted us enough for us to arrange the stop. Why don't you trust us enough to be straight with us?" Ricky responded, "Hey look, I trust you guys. Hell, I like you. That's one of the reasons they sent me to work with you. They know I have a high opinion of your group. They also know Val and I go back a long way and we have made some good cases together." Jimmy asked, "So the issue is with Doug?" Ricky then told they guys looking each one of them in the eye, "You said, not me. And I would like to remind you, I don't want to have to leave my wife and child to go get killed in the desert. I made it out of there once. My luck may have run out." Brent said, "Oh, you don't have to worry about us say anything. We're not like that. We can be trusted, and we do what we say we are going to do."

Ricky said, "That's fair, I deserve that one on behalf of Doug. I told you I'm going to be completely honest with you, and I am. I just did by passing along this information. You gotta give me credit for that."

Val closed out the conversation with, "Okay Ricky, we'll take your word for it. But you shouldn't hold it against us if we're a little apprehensive about things going forward." Ricky replied, "Look, I don't blame you. This is disappointing. You should have been in on the plans, and you weren't. To be totally transparent, neither was I. I'll ask more questions of my own group in the future. Things will get better one way or the other."

Brent said, "Well, you buy the beer and we'll think about it."

Chapter 12 Johnny Spots a Plate

The wire traffic had been slow since the produce truck was stopped and sent rolling down the highway. The Hernandez Cartel decided to lay low for a few weeks. This is the part of narcotics work that Brent disliked, hour after hour of waiting for either some information from the field, or other agencies, or an informant. It seemed like time just dragged by and the days went by slowly with apparently nothing being done.

Doug entered the wire room and asked Val about recent calls, "Have you heard anything interesting lately? Are there aren't any calls that sound like they're moving again? I'm tired of sitting around here doing nothing. I know the guys on the road are getting bored too."

Val sighed and said, "No, they seem a little spooked since that produce truck was stopped. One of the guys in Mexico talked about not crossing for a while. Even the number of calls has slowed down. Phone records show the targets near San Antonio have been calling the targets in Mexico, but the guys in Mexico aren't answering. They call each other in Mexico, but they're very cautious about what they say. Most of the conversations involve asking each other what they think is responsible for the trailer stop."

Doug asked, "What's your guess, Val. Do they have an opinion on the subject?" Val replied, "They don't know what to think. Some of them say they think it was just bad luck. Some of them buy the story the officers gave about it being a DOT stop. Others wonder if the stop was the result of a snitch in San Antonio or Dallas. They go back and forth on it. You never know what they're going to come up with." Doug said, "If they're trying to root out the snitch, there may be some bodies found in San Antonio or Dallas. The cartel may have a meeting and decide who needs to go. I'd sure hate to be one of the new guys involved in either one of those cities. You know how they act, if they point the finger at someone, he just disappears."

Val said, "I guess it's possible, but I don't think it's come to that yet. I haven't heard them talking about anyone. I don't think anyone is in imminent danger. If they end up with somebody specific in mind, I'll let you know. It shouldn't be that tough. When they're talking about a person, they'll use a real name or a nickname. I've got some people identified between the phone logs and the nicknames. They talk about people like, Chico, Wero or Prieto, names like that." Doug was getting excited about the prospects and instructed, "Listen close to that kind of thing. If we do get information about a possible hit and we know it is, maybe we can talk to them and get them to flip. You know, pick him up and tell him their bosses are about to kill them. Sometimes that will make the guy changes his loyalties. Everybody knows how ruthless these animals are. I mean, if they put a green light on me, I'd tell the feds anything they want to hear, especially if they could give me a name change and a new place to live. Do me a big favor and put me in the protective witness program."

Brent walked in to the wire room as Doug was walking out. Brent pulled up a chair next to Val's and started reading some of Val's notes. Val had his headphones on and was listening to another call. Brent's phone rang and he answered, "Hello." The voice on the other line said, "Brent, it's Johnny. It took me a while to get around to telling you so, but I'm really sorry about what happened to Harry." Brent replied, "Yeah, we all are. What's going on Skinny Johnny?"

Johnny said, "First of all, I want to thank you for the payment on that case involving the money. I never expected to get fifty thousand dollars!" Brent said, "Well you deserved it. We never expected to recover a million dollars either. Fifty thousand was a fair payment." Johnny continued in his usual "Hustle and Jive" style, "Hey bro, I think I got something good. I was partying with some friends the other night at Planeta Mexico. I ran into Eddie Coronado. Do you know who he is?" Brent asked, "No, who is he?" Johnny continued, "Dude, he's the youngest son of the Coronado family. The word is they are moving Hernandez coke. Hernandez brings in the coke for the biggest part of the San Antonio supply. I can't believe you don't know who he is." Brent became agitated, "Well, excuse the shit out of me. Hold on, hey Val, do you know who the Coronado family is? Johnny's talking to me about a guy named Eddie Coronado." Val looked at Brent, removed the headphones and asked, "What are you talking about? I couldn't hear you." Brent asked, "Do you know the Coronado family? Johnny says they move a lot of coke here." Val replied, "Oh yeah that's true. But I think they're all in federal prison. Mingo and I made a case on Henry Coronado fifteen years ago. He's doing life for trafficking." Brent turned his attention back to the phone and said, "Val says he knows them, but they are all in federal prison." Johnny replied, "Yeah, Val's thinking about the grandpa and this guy Eddies' dad. The old man's son is Junior. The guy I saw at the bar the other nights name is Eddie. Eddie is Junior's son. This kid Eddie is the only one from the Coronado family not in prison. Some of the guys I know in the Mexican Mafia say Eddie's an idiot. The Hernandez are supposed to have a guy living with him to handle the shipments as they come in. The roommate is a guy from Mexico. He's the one that gets the kilos out to some pretty big dealers."

Brent being at his usual suspicious self-asked, "Johnny, it doesn't sound like they need this guy, Eddie. Why would they let an idiot be involved if a guy from the cartel is doing all the work?"

Johnny replied, "They say the old man was pretty good friends with Daniel Hernandez. You know, the old man, number one. I've heard they did business together in the seventies. Hernandez would send loads from Mexico to San Antonio. Coronado would receive the shipments here. Letting Eddie be involved is like a little gift to the Coronado family. The Coronado family has a distribution system in place in San Antonio. Eddie doesn't make any of the decisions, but the system the Coronado's have is valuable.

The cartel gets to use a system that's twenty years old. That's why they let a dumbass like Eddie be involved." Brent asked, "Okay, you talked to Eddie and you're pretty sure he's involved in the trafficking. Do you know where he lives?" "No", replied Johnny. Brent then asked, "Do you know what he's driving?"

Johnny was now feeling good about his proposition, and then threw in his most important information, "Yeah, it's a brand-new Mercedes two door. I got the license plate number too." Brent being more cautious asked, "So, you saw a guy in a bar that's supposed to be a crook, and you got a plate. What am I supposed to do with that? Call me when you know where I can find him. Do you know where he lives?" The shoe was now on the other foot with Johnny and he was showing his frustration, "Damn Brent, you're getting as bad as the DEA. Do you want me to go out and find him, then cuff him? Okay, I'll arrest him and bring him to you."

There was silence on the phone for a few seconds as both men contemplated where this conversation was headed then Johnny spoke up, "Okay, I'm sorry about that, man. Let me tell you what happened. I do have a plate. The other night when the club closed, he and I walked through the parking lot together. My car was parked behind his. As he drove off, I wrote down the plate number. I thought about following him, but I didn't want to get caught doing that. I didn't know whether the guy staying with him was at this place or not. I mean, if what I heard is true, he could be pretty dangerous." Brent replied, "Okay Johnny, now you're starting to get a little interesting. I thought maybe you called to give me a lesson in the history of drug trafficking in San Antonio. Or maybe you just called to give me some crap." Johnny said, "Okay Brent, I said I was sorry. I thought maybe you can figure out where he lives with the plate number. The car he got into was a brand-new Mercedes. You know, one of those little two door sports cars. I don't know what it's worth, but it looked really expensive."

Brent told Johnny, "I doubt we'll figure out where he lives from the registration of the plate. No doper with any sense allows his address to go on the registration. They know that would make it too easy to find them." Johnny said, "Well, this guy isn't exactly Einstein. He won't be splitting atoms anytime soon. You never know, maybe you'll get lucky." Brent replied, "Okay Johnny, I'll let you know what we figure out." Brent hung up the phone and turned to a computer to run Eddie's license plate number. Sure enough, the car was registered to, Eduardo Coronado. The home address was a very expensive apartment complex on the far north side of San Antonio. Brent turned to Val said, "Johnny says Juniors' son is an idiot named Eddie. He's supposed to be running their portion of the coke through San Antonio. I know he's an idiot because he drives around in a new Mercedes with the registration in his name, what a fool."

Val asked, "If he's an idiot, why would he be in charge?" Brent explained, "Johnny says Eddie's the only Coronado not in prison. He also says Eddie's not calling the shots but there is supposed to be a Hernandez cartel member handling the distribution. Do you think what Johnny's saying could be true?" Val replied, "I don't know, Brent. But the Coronado's have been doing business in San Antonio for decades. If there is one of the family members involved, it could be a pretty big deal. It's worth checking out. Does Johnny know where Eddie lives?" Brent replied, "That's the crazy part, the plate checks out. It comes back to an Eduardo Coronado. The address is to a fancy apartment complex on the northside of town. The apartment is just inside the city limits. It's the only apartment complex in that area. I've never even seen it. It's at the foothills of the hill country."

Val thought about it for a minute and said, "I'm caught up on all the calls. It's been really slow for the last few days. Let's go out to that apartment complex and see if we can find the car. I wouldn't think he would be using his home address, but you never know, he might just be that stupid. Let's go find out"

Brent said, "I think we should. Johnny's been on a hot streak with his information. If it's Hernandez -related, I'm interested. Should we tell Ricky about it and take him with us?" Val said, "I don't know, did Doug tell us he was going to put a tracker on that trailer? I think we just keep this to ourselves. We don't have anything yet."

Brent and Val drove to the apartment complex and found a two door Mercedes parked in front of building twelve. The license plate number matched the one Johnny gave Brent. They parked in a spot where they could see the Mercedes and the front doors of the building. Brent looked at Val and said, "Well, so far so good. I can't believe the Mercedes is here. Maybe he's just visiting. I think this is worth putting some time in, don't you?" Val replied, "Oh yeah, it couldn't happen at a better time. I'm caught up on the calls. I'll tell Doug I'm going to take a couple of days off from the wire room since it's so slow right now. He shouldn't have a problem with it. I've been in that damn room for a month now without a break. We'll watch Eddie for a few days and see what he's doing." Brent said to himself, "Finally back to doing some actual police work and not riding a desk, this might turn out to be something".

For the second day after finding Eddie Coronado's Mercedes, Val and Brent were sitting in the parking lot watching Eddie's car. Over the two days they did see some movement and documented it with photos and videos. They saw Eddie come and go from the apartment doing routine things. They watched him go to lunch, they watch him go to the grocery store and they watched him go to bars at night. But they hadn't seen him do anything that looked suspicious. At the beginning of the third day, Brent looked at Val and asked, "Well, what do you think? I don't think we're going to see him carrying boxes into the apartment. So far, the only thing we've learned is where he likes to buy his groceries and which bar, he likes to hang out in."

Val thought about it for a few seconds, sighed and said, "I think we could watch him for another week and not learn anything. I'm going back into the wire room tomorrow. We need to close this thing out today, one way or the other. If we get him stopped on the road, maybe we'll find something in the car. Or maybe he'll say, you caught me. I've got an apartment full of dope. We'll let him get a long way from the apartment before stopping him. We'll act like we don't know where he's coming from during the interview. If he doesn't want to talk about the apartment, we'll probably be onto something. If he does admit to living in the apartment, I guess were out of luck and we've wasted three days watching him. But I've wasted three days watching a lesser target before. Let's give it a shot. Why don't you call the guys and get them out here?"

Brent got on his radio and said, "Mingo, Jimmy, why don't you come out here to Eddie's apartment. We're going to close this thing out today. We could use some help with mobile surveillance." Mingo, always able to see things clearly in hindsight said, "Isn't that what I said we should do two days ago? I guess you're finally seeing things my way. If you guys would listen to me, you wouldn't waste so much time." Brent said, "Yeah, yeah, yeah, you're a damned genius. Now, why don't you get your old ass out here and bring Jimmy with you? See if you can line us up a patrolman for a traffic stop. That is, if you can break away from solitaire or shopping or whatever it is, you're doing." Mingo replied, "Now that's just plain rude to your elders, boy. I'll come out there and see if you and Val are on the right track. I'll line up a patrolman, just don't screw this thing up before I get there."

An hour after Jimmy, Mingo and the patrolman joined Val and Brent across from the apartment complex, Eddie walked out of his apartment and got into his car. Brent and Val had an eye on the apartment. Brent got on his radio and said, "Ok boys, here we go. He just got in his car and he's driving toward the front gate. Just hang back a few blocks as we leave." Hearing the activity, the patrolman said, "I'll be out of sight until you're ready for the stop."

Brent said, "That sounds great, he's headed out the front gate and onto the access road of IH 37. It looks like he's going to be headed south on IH 37 toward downtown. Let's just follow a while longer until he gets further away from the apartment. I don't want him to know we've been on him the whole time." Mingo on the police radio and said, "We're behind you Brent, and the patrolman is behind us." Brent replied, "Okay, I think we're far enough away from the apartment to get him stopped. Patrol, would you come up and watch him from a distance? Wait till you see a traffic violation to make the stop. That shouldn't be hard to do, he's over the speed limit and weaving in and out of traffic. Come on up and stop him for speeding. If we don't do it now, he might get away from us." The patrolman replied, "Okay, I'm coming up fast now. I think I see him. Is that him in the middle lane?" Brent replied, "Yep, that's him, go ahead and get him pulled over in a good spot."

The officer waited until the highway had a large shoulder where the interview could take place in a safe place. The patrol cars light bar came on with red and blue lights flashing, the Mercedes pulled over onto the shoulder. Brent got on the radio and said, "Tell him he was speeding, write the ticket and asked for permission to search the car. We'll cover you just out of sight." "Okay, I'll get back on the radio and let you know what we got" replied the patrolman. Brent, Val, Mingo and Jimmy watched as the patrol officer approached the Mercedes stopped in front of the patrol car. Without hearing a word, they knew the officer was asking for his license and insurance paperwork. They saw Eddie hand the officer his driver's license and proof of insurance. They watched the officer go back and get into his patrol car. Then the silence was broken by the patrolman's radio call, "I've got Eduardo Coronado driving the car. His driver's license shows an address of 1044 S. San Gabriel." Val and Brent were excited. Val said, "That's his dad's address!" Brent said, "It's looking good. Go ahead and write him the ticket and ask him for permission to search the vehicle." "10-4" replied the patrolman. The narc's watched anxiously as the officer again approached the car. The patrolman asked Eddie, "Do you have anything illegal in the car?" Eddie said, "No, you can search it if you want to." The patrolman stated, "Thank you, sir. Would you please get out of the car and stand to the side of the road?" "Sure, no problem" replied Eddie. Eddie got out of the car and did as he was asked. The officer only searched for a few seconds. He raised the top of the center console and found a plastic bag containing orange oval-shaped tablets. He retrieved the plastic bag, walked to the back of the car and held the bag high in the air so Val and Brent could see he found something suspicious. Brent said, "He's got something, Val. Let's drive up there." Brent put the car in gear and drove the short distance to the traffic stop.

Still trying to conceal their intentions from Eddie, Brent and Val walked up to the car. Val said, "Hello officer, I'm with the narcotics office." As he held his badge up for the officer and Eddie to see. "We were driving by and I was wondering if you needed any help?" The patrol officer said, "Boy, I'm glad you're here. I just found this bag of pills in this guy's car. I don't know what they are. Can you help me with this?" Val looked at Eddie, and then back at the officer and said, "I think we can help you. Did you ask him what they are?" The patrolman replied, "No, I was just about to when you drove up." The officer then turned to Eddie, held up the bag for him to see and asked, "What kind of pills these?"

Eddie replied, "I don't know. I let people borrow my car all the time. That's not mine. Someone must have left that in here." Val looked at Brent and said, "Brent, would you call poison control and figure out what these are?" Brent replied, "Sure Val, I can do that." Brent took the bag of pills and walked back toward his car and got on the phone. He called poison control, described the pill to the agent, and learned the pills were Xanax. Brent walked back to where the three men were standing and told Val, "These are Xanax. It's a controlled substance. But they're not in a legal container and I don't see a prescription." Val looked at Eddie and said, "Well Eddie, it seems you're in illegal possession of a controlled substance. Do you have a prescription for these pills?" Eddie responded defiantly, "I do, I just don't have it with me." Val explained, "Well, you may not know it, but if you're in possession of a controlled substance it has to be contained in the bottle it was

prescribed in." Eddie said, "The bottle is at home. I just poured some in this bag to take them with me."
Val said, "Didn't you just tell me a few minutes ago these weren't yours and you didn't know where they came from? Now you're saying they are yours and you don't have the bottle with you. Which is it, are they yours are not?" Eddie knew he was caught in a lie replied, "Yeah they're mine. I just didn't understand what you are asking a minute ago." Val stated, "Well, since they are yours, you are in violation of the controlled substance act."

Eddie laughed and said, "Ok, narc, you caught me. I have been trying to hide this terrible crime from you cops for years. Now you made a big bust. I guess you can go back to your office and tell your buddies what a big case you made." Val and Brent smiled. Brent then looked at the patrol officer and said, "I heard you calling him Eddie. What's his full name?" The officer looked at Eddie's driver's license again and said, "His name is, Eduardo Coronado." After the officer handed Val Eddie's driver's license, Val said, "Look here Brent, Eddie Coronado has an address on South San Gabriel. I used to know a Coronado family that lived on San Gabriel. Of course, I thought they were all in prison." Val turned to Eddie and asked, "Is your father and your grandfather in federal prison?" Eddie was getting angry that his family history was now being put out in the open and asked, "Yeah, they are, so what?" Val replied, "I just learned something. Not all of the Coronado's are in prison." Eddie said, "Yeah, you learned something. It seems like you got a lot to learn." Normally, Brent and Val would have been angry about such a wise ass remark. But they were happy about this one. Val asked, "Mr. Eddie Coronado, where are you coming from?" "I'm coming from my house on San Gabriel" replied Eddie. "Val asked, "So, you live on San Gabriel?" Becoming more and more agitated Eddie replied, "Yeah, I live on San Gabriel. What kind of detective are you? You're standing there with my driver's license in your hand and asked me where I live? You're not all that smart, are you?" Calmly and coolly Val asked, "So, you live on San Gabriel? Eddie replied, "You got it, Colombo." Val said, "You're a very funny guy, Eddie. I may know more about you than you think. For example, I know you just left your apartment on the north side. Now, I ask you, is that funny?" Looking confused Eddie asked, "Apartment, what apartment?" Brent had all he could take of Eddie's belligerence and said, "Okay Eddie, the fun is all over now. We're going to get a warrant to search your apartment." Eddie asked, "A warrant to search my apartment? A warrant for what?"

Val and Brent both laughed, and Brent said, "There you go again. Didn't you just tell us you don't live in an apartment? Eddie, you changed the address on your driver's license but not the car registration." Eddie dropped his head and said, "Damn!"

Val got on his radio and said, "Jimmy, go back to the office and type out a warrant for Eddie's apartment. Make the warrant for illegal possession of Xanax. It'll make a good warrant and get us in the door. Who knows what we'll find after that?" Jimmy typed up an affidavit, presented it to a municipal court judge and got it signed. He was back to the scene of the car stop in an hour.

With a warrant in hand, Val showed the warrant to Eddie who was now seated in the back of a patrol car. Val said, "Eddie, here's the warrant. Do you have anything you want to tell me?" "Yeah, I do" said Eddie. "What is it Eddie?" asked Val. Eddie started to confess, "There's some stuff in there." Val continued his questioning, "What kind of stuff? Is there dope in your apartment?" Eddie replied, "Yeah, there's coke." Val asked, "How much coke?" Eddie said, "A lot." Val continued, "How much is a lot?" Eddie stated, "I don't know, fifteen or twenty kilos." Val and Brent were stunned by what they heard. When Val regained the ability to speak again without stuttering, he asked, "Is there money?" Eddie replied, "Yeah, there's money. A lot of money." Val asked, "How much is a lot?" Eddie said "I don't know. I think there's about a million." Brent didn't mean to say anything during Val's interrogation but involuntarily said, "Oh, shit!" Val turned to Brent with a straight face and said, "Maybe we should go back to the apartment right now." Brent told Jimmy and Mingo, "Follow us, we're going to the apartment."

They parked in front of Eddie's apartment. Eddie was in the backseat of the patrol car. Val opened the back door of the patrol car and asked Eddie, "Is there anyone in the apartment?" Eddie replied, "No, the guy that stays with me is in Mexico. Just don't break the door, the keys are in my pocket." Val took a set of keys out of Eddie's pocket. Val, Brent, Jimmy and Mingo walked to the door. They used a key to unlock and open the door. They searched the apartment and found no one inside. Brent walked into the main bedroom and opened the door to the walk-in closet. He saw thirty bundles of what he believed was kilos of cocaine. He also saw a "Coach" brand, duffel bag on the floor. Brent unzipped the bag and saw it was full of bills. Stacks of one hundred-dollar bills. In a daze, Brent walked back into the living room and saw the other three detectives. Brent said, "There's kilos in the closet and a duffel bag full of money. The bundles of money looked like nothing but hundred-dollar bills." All four men walked back to the room and stared into the closet. It was hard to believe what they saw. The patrol officer walked Eddie back into the apartment and set him on the couch. Brent, Val, Mingo, Jimmy and the officer stood in front of Eddie. Eddie asked Val, "Can I have one of those Xanax? I could really use one." Val said, "Well, I'm not supposed to, but I know what you mean. I could use one too. Do you have more in the house?" Eddie replied, "Yeah, I've got some above the sink." Val checked the cabinet above the sink and found a prescription bottle of Xanax. The label on the bottle showed Eddie did have a prescription for Xanax. Val handed Eddie one with a glass of water. Val looked at Brent and said, "I guess we better call Ricky. After all, he is a part of our group." Brent asked, "What are we going to tell him?" Val said, "We're going to tell him exactly what happened. This fine officer made a stop for speeding. He found a bag of Xanax in the car. We were driving by and asked him if he needed help. We volunteered our help and it led to this." Brent with a big smile on his face asked, "I like it, Val. Do you think Doug is going to be heated up?" Val laughed and said,

"Heated up, I think his hair will be on fire. I think we better get ready for another talking to from the captain."

It just goes to show how much "loyalty" goes between departments involved in the "war against drugs". Val looked at the score between the PD group and the DEA as, one to one going into the middle innings.

Chapter 13   It Hits the Fan

After the PD group made the case on Eddie Coronado, Ricky was required to write a DEA report covering his involvement in the case. His involvement was minimal, but DEA standard operating procedure requires documentation of an agent's actions. He handed the report to his supervisor, Doug Garland. Doug looked over the report at the San Antonio DEA Headquarters and asked, "What the hell is this?"

Ricky knowing that Doug was about to hit the roof said quietly, "The PD guys made a case on a local trafficker, named Eddie Coronado. By the time I got there, everything was pretty much said and done. But I did make the scene, so I thought I'd better write you a report." Doug told Ricky, "Sit down, let me look at this thing." It only took Doug about 15 seconds before he glared at Ricky and asked, "Did you know they were working on this?" Ricky replied, "No, they called me after they were in the apartment." This news absolutely ticked off Doug, he asked, "So they didn't involve you in this at all? They just did it on their own? I thought we were supposed to be working together. I think they kept you out of it on purpose. Those guys are trying to do things on their own."

Ricky had dealt with Doug many times before when he had become bitter and angry and knew that he did not want to escalate the conversation and said, "I don't believe that. It all started as the result of a traffic stop. A patrolman stopped Coronado and found Xanax in his car. The patrolman called for assistance from narcotics and they went out to help him. One thing led to another, and they ended up in his apartment and found the coke and the money."

 Doug was incredulous, "Do you really believe that crock of shit? I don't believe it happened like that. I bet they made the whole thing up and didn't call you for a reason." Ricky continued to try to deflate the hostility, "I have no reason to doubt them. These kinds of cases happen all the time as the result of a traffic stop. I think it was just good luck. Some of our best cases were based on luck. What are you telling me, you're going to hold good luck against them? Some of the dope has the Hernandez emblem on it, but I don't think it had anything to do with Hernandez when it started." Doug then continued to make his case, "Well let's see, Val wanted a couple of days off from the wire room. He didn't take his wife on vacation. He didn't go fishing. He didn't spend three days on a golf course. He just happened to make a case on the Hernandez Cartel, and you think that's just good luck?" Ricky replied, "I have to admit, it seems like quite a coincidence. But I'm not going to question them on it. After all, they did keep us updated and I think that's what's expected from two different agencies working together. You know, just like we had them in the loop on the trailer." Leaning back in his chair and visibly angry, Doug said, "Oh, so it's my fault they didn't include you on this?" Ricky said, "I'm not saying it's your fault. I'm just saying I can understand why they might play it a little close to the vest. Besides, these guys have been doing narcotics work for a long time. Val and Mingo were making street cases long before you and I were agents. I think it's wrong to believe just because they're a local group, they're not smart enough to make a big case." Doug continued, "Well I'm glad to see how understanding you are with them, because I'm taking you off this case and assigning you to administrative duty. Do you remember what that's like? You're going to be doing our prescription cases. So, go out there and find you a comfortable chair because you won't be leaving the office for a long time. You'll get thirty minutes for lunch, other than that you'll be in here. As a matter of fact, I don't need your PD buddies anymore either. I'm going to call the chief of police and let him know how his detectives are damaging our case." Ricky was livid, "Damaging your case, they got this case started to begin with and they lost a friend in the process! If your theory about them intentionally going out and knocking off a big load of dope and money is right, remember, they've got a pretty good informant. Cutting them out will mean cutting the informant out too. You can make me stay in the office, but you can't make them stay in their office." Doug stood up behind his desk and asked, "What are you still doing in my office? You probably have a thousand prescription cases waiting for you out there. Now get the hell out of my office and start typing up paper work on a silly ass script case."

On the following day, the PD group was removed from the Hernandez cartel investigation per orders of the Chief of Police. Except for Skinny Johnny, most of the informants had been put on hold. The PD detective's attention was focused on trying to move the Hernandez case forward. Sgt. Clower came out of his office to have roll call. He told the guys, "Wayne just called me, he needs a couple of guys to help with a search warrant. The daylight sergeant said Wayne and Dave could stay late to run the warrant, but they need to get some help from the evening shift. Any volunteers?" Brent said, "I ate before I came in. I'll go help them." Val also volunteered, "Me too, I'll go with Brent. It's not like I have a wire room waiting for me." Sgt. Clower said, "Okay, give Wayne a call. I guess he'll tell you where to meet them."

Val and Brent rode in the same car. They headed toward the pre-arranged meeting spot at a church on the westside of San Antonio. When they got there, they found Wayne and Dave waiting. Brent looked at Val and said, "Wayne and I use to work patrol together. When I went to homicide, he went to daylight narcotics. Every time I saw him, he would tell me how much fun he was having. At the time, I never imagined he would be working daylight, and I would be working the evening shift. I've always called him, Wayne the pain." Val asked, "Wayne the pain, why Wayne the pain?" Brent explained, "Wayne has a special, go-to move when he's in a fight. When things aren't going his way, he kind of makes a peace sign with the index and middle finger of his right hand. Then he takes that peace sign and jams two fingers in his opponents' eyes. You know, kind of like the Three Stooges. Maybe that's where he picked it up, watching the Three Stooges." Val said, "Oh I love that move. I used to use it too, but I never actually stuck it in anyone's eyes. I just used it like I was going to poke my cousin's eyes and say, yuk, yuk, yuk." Brent continued, "Well, when Wayne does it, he's not faking anything. I've seen him do it couple of times and I thought he was going to bring out brain matter on the ends of those fingers. It's incredible, I can't believe the guys he's done it to aren't blinded. I mean, except for the screaming the recipients do when the fingers plunge into the eyes, they seem to recover pretty quickly. I suppose there's the possibility of nightmares for the rest of their lives. They should make a video of it. They could run it on some sort of medical show. It would be proof of how resilient the eyes are." Val asked, "Does he do it every time he's in a fight?" Brent replied, "No, I think it's held in reserve just for emergencies."

As Val and Brent drove into the parking lot, Wayne and Dave were getting their raid gear out of the trunk of Wayne's car. Brent got out of the passenger seat of Val's car and said, "Well if it ain't old Wayne the pain. Why are you guys bothering us with one of your smalltime warrants? Couldn't you find some small-time daylight guys to help?" Wayne said, "Oh, that chicken shit Sgt. of mine wouldn't let any of the daylight guys stay to help. He's scared to death they're going to get some overtime. The way he treats overtime, you'd think it was coming out of his pocket." Brent asked, "Do you have a patrolman on the way?" Dave said, "Yeah, I asked for one. He should be on the way. This shouldn't be a big deal. If it wasn't for SOP's requiring one, we'd just do it ourselves. But I guess it never hurts to have a uniformed presence." Val said, "I guess having a uniformed presence probably started when Mingo ran a warrant a couple of years ago. They got in a shootout. After it was over, the crook testified he was afraid and said he thought he was being robbed. He said guys were coming in the door with guns and he was terrified. He didn't see anyone that looked like a policeman. I was shocked he got off the rap that easy."

The patrol car pulled into the church parking with a young patrolman at the wheel. Now that everyone involved was at the meet spot, Wayne briefed the group "There shouldn't be anything to this one. There's only supposed to be one guy in the house. I don't have any information about guns, but the informant said he's been in the house lots of times and didn't see any. There's not supposed to be in any dog's either. Like I said, it should be pretty easy." Wayne looked at the patrolman and said, "Just follow in behind us. The house is only a few blocks away." He then looked at Val and Brent and said, "I'll hit the door, Dave will go in first, Brent second, then Val and I'll go in behind him." Wayne again went over the instructions to the patrolman, "After we get in, you can come in behind us. Everything should be calm by then. Okay, let's go."

Wayne's car led the way to the target house. Val's car was behind Wayne's, and the patrol car was in the rear. The cars made a few turns while driving, then stopped about 20 feet away from the target house. Wayne got out of his car and retrieved the battering ram from the trunk. Dave followed Wayne, Brent and Val followed Dave. The patrolman was a few steps behind Val. The four detectives quietly stepped up on the tall wooden front porch of the old house. Holding the ram about waist high, Wayne looked back making sure everyone was in position. Then Wayne planted his feet, drew the ram back and slammed it into the doorknob. There was a huge bang when the ram hit the door, but the door didn't open. It didn't even move much. Wayne swung the ram hitting the door again with the same result, nothing. The door looked about the same as it did when they got there.

The narcotics detectives knew from previous experience the door had to be barricaded. They also knew the element of surprise was lost. The danger level skyrocketed when the door didn't open immediately. If there was a crook inside, he had plenty of time to prepare for the officers who were trying to make entry.

 Over and over, Wayne slammed the ram into the door. The anxiety of not getting in quickly played a part in Brent's decision to stand directly in front of the door. As Wayne hit the door over and over, the door would open a few inches and then immediately slam shut. This happened time after time. Brent could see into the house for a split second when the door would open a few inches then close again. After four or five times, something about the interior of the house looked familiar to Brent. His brain was getting just enough information for the image to look familiar. But not enough information to determine what he was seeing. After seeing the same images, over and over, Brent finally figured it out. He was seeing a man about ten feet inside the door standing with a shotgun held ready at the hip.

Brent assumed the man was about to shoot through the front door. Brent yelled, "Gun!" Just after Brent yelled, gun, he saw the explosion of a muzzle flash from the interior of the house. Wayne jumped off the left side of the porch just as the gun was fired. Brent jumped off the right side into the yard.

As Wayne fell to the left, he drew his pistol and started firing into the house. First through the front door, then the wall. Dave had the same idea at the same time and joined Wayne in the gunfire. The .40 caliber rounds penetrate easily through the door and the wall on the left side of the door. Brent knew he had to get off the porch and away from the shotgun blasts. He didn't have time to draw his pistol. Brent jumped off the porch and ran to the front right corner of the house. He looked back toward the door and saw Val laying in the yard about half way between the porch and the corner of the house.

Brent ran back to Val and picked him up. As Val got to his feet, he limped toward the right side of the house. Brent saw Val limping and yelled, "Are you hit?" Val yelled, "No you big son of a bitch, you stepped on me!" As Brent bailed off the porch moving to the right, he knocked Val off the porch and into the yard and didn't even know it. As Brent was tending to Val, he didn't hear the shooter inside screaming, "I'm down, I'm down." But Wayne and Dave did.

Wayne and Dave cautiously made their way back onto the porch. The shotgun blasts went through the doorknob and the locking mechanism of the door. The door was opened by the buck shot and now stood open about a foot. Wayne peaked into the house very carefully. He could see the man who shot through the door was lying face down on the living room floor. His arms were stretched out to both sides. Wayne and Dave entered the house.

Standing on the right side of the house, Brent saw Dave and Wayne going in through the door. After not hearing the man inside giving up, Brent said out loud, "Oh, these guys are crazy." But reluctantly, Brent followed the other two into the house. As Brent stepped inside the door, he was relieved to see that Dave and Wayne were upright, and the shooter was face down on the floor. It was finally time to take a breath. Wayne looked at Brent and asked, "Are you alright? Brent replied still catching his breath, "Yeah, I'm fine. "Wayne didn't see Val and with great concern asked, "Where's Val, is he, all right?" Brent said, "Yeah he's alright, he's out there in the front yard with a sore leg." Wayne was sure Val was shot and asked, "How bad is it?" Brent laughed when he realized Wayne's concern and said, "Oh, he's not shot. I guess I stepped on him jumping off the porch." Nervous laughter broke out between Brent, Dave and Wayne as they stood over the shooter.

Now that things were over, Brent had a chance to look around. Then it occurred to him, he didn't see the patrolman. He asked Wayne, "Where's our uniformed helper?" Wayne and Dave were busy trying to get their prisoner to his feet and didn't even hear the question. Worried about the officer being shot, Brent hurried back out to the front yard and looked around. Brent found Val in the front yard and asked, "Have you seen the patrolman?" Val said, "No, I haven't seen the patrolman. I think you broke my leg, stupid ass." Brent thought about how funny Val was, hopping around on his sore leg. Val was still angry. Brent said, "Oh you'll be alright, just to rub some dirt on it." Then Brent laughed hysterically. Val, who is more apt to be working a wire or any less physical activity replied, "It's not funny, you gorilla looking bastard." Brent said, "Okay, okay, I just thought it was funny, that's all."

Brent's attention turned back to find the patrolman. He didn't see him in the yard. He figured the patrolman must have followed them up to the front of the house when they tried to make entry. Brent walked out to the street and saw the patrol car parked behind theirs. He looked down the street in the other direction. Under a streetlight about five houses down, Brent saw the patrolman's badge flashing in the light.

Brent was relieved. He waved his arm toward the patrolman trying to get him to come back to the house. When the patrolman got back, he was animated and angry. It occurred to Brent the patrolman ran when the shooting started, and Brent laughed. The patrolman was made angrier by Brent's laughter. The patrolman said, "I thought you told me this was going to be easy. You said the guy in the house didn't have any guns. Are you a bunch of dumb asses or what?" Brent was still amused by the whole thing. He looked at the patrolman who was furious about being involved in his first shooting case. Brent walked back into the house and looked around.

Brent wondered where the bullets fired by Wayne and Dave ended up. He walked into the kitchen and saw holes in the refrigerator. He then looked over at a washer and dryer and saw holes in them too. Brent again laughed hysterically. Wayne looked at Brent and asked, "What the hell are you laughing at?" Brent told Wayne, "Boy, you and Dave sure hate appliances, don't you?"

All in all, things went well. No one was really hurt, except for Val's minor leg injury. Wayne and Dave made a good case. During the trial the homeowner said was trying to defend his home and 3 kg of tar heroin from the intruders. During cross-prosecution, the defendant said he didn't know the people knocking down his door were policeman. He thought the people trying to get in the front door were there to rob him. Nice try, that's why they bring a uniformed officer with them, even if he ends up running down the street in fear. The defendant was convicted for possession of a controlled substance.

Chapter 14 Ricky Explains

Val and Brent were having lunch when Val got a phone call. On the other line was their old DEA friend Ricky. The voice on the line said, "Hey son, it's Ricky. What are you boys up to?" Val said, "Brent and I are just having some lunch. Jimmy and Mingo are down at the land cut near Port Mansfield doing some fishing. What are you up to? Ricky said, "Oh, I just haven't talked to you and Brent in a while. I thought we might meet tonight for a beer." Val replied, "Well, that will work out great. Brent and I were just saying we didn't have anything going. We thought we'd be at Hills and Dales about seven. I think you're aware of the table where we will be sitting." Ricky said, "Oh, yeah, I know the table. I believe we've put away two or three hundred cases of beer sitting at that table. Sounds good. I look forward to seeing you guys."

At seven o'clock, Brent and Val walked in to the beer joint. While they were getting their first beer, they saw Ricky standing at a table full of young ladies, laying on his southern charm. When they walked up to the table, Ricky told the ladies, "Excuse me girls, my friends have just arrived. As you can see, we're a group of good-looking men. I hope to talk to you later." Ricky shook hands with Val and Brent and then said, "Let's go out to y'all's favorite table." Val said, "I don't know about going out to our table, it's a little cool outside. Brent doesn't have his heavy panties on. "

Ricky explained, "Well, I got some news. It's not necessarily great news. I thought you and Brent might want the opportunity to holler at me a little. I didn't want to disturb the other drunks in here." Val shook his head in anticipation of the bad news. They walked out the back door and sat at their usual table under the big oak tree. Ricky said, "You know what Mingo told me one time? He said he brought Brent to this table when he and Brent first started riding together. I thought it was a pretty good story." Val said, "Yeah, that's a good story. But I don't think you wanted to meet us here to talk about the history of this table. Let's hear it Ricky." Ricky said, "Don't freak out now. I got a little bad news, but I also wanted to give you something I thought you might be able to use." While staring at Ricky, Brent said, "I always like to hear the bad news first." Ricky took a deep breath and said, "Of course you remember the produce trailer from Laredo that ended up in Dallas. Well, Dallas wasn't the only place it stopped. Three agents followed the truck and trailer to Dallas, Philadelphia and New York. It started coming back south and made a stop in Atlanta. It was there for about a week. It was only in the other two cities a day or so. The guys were watching that truck since it left San Antonio. Something different was happening in Atlanta. In the other cities, they saw produce coming off the trailer. But in Atlanta it was parked for almost a week. They watched as guys went in and out of the trailer. But they weren't taking pallets of produce out, they were taking hand carried bundles in. When they walked out of the trailer, they weren't carrying anything. Clearly in Atlanta they weren't unloading, they were loading. Surveillance figured they were loading money to go back to Mexico.

The agents doing the surveillance had the truck stopped on IH 35 near Pearsall headed south. DPS made the traffic stop. Then they took it to a police yard in Pearsall. They searched the trailer and found the money. A lot of money. The total was 1.75 million." Val asked, "One and three-quarter million dollars? Did that money drive through San Antonio before it got to Pearsall? "Ricky said,

"Yes Val, it did. It came in to San Antonio on IH 10 from Atlanta. Then headed back south on IH 35."

Val said, "So, the information that I picked out on the wire was used to find the truck. Our guys were in on the surveillance of the truck. Brent lined up the traffic stop and SAPD traffic made the stop. Brent asked, "Did they wait for it to get out of San Antonio to spite us?" Ricky explained, "It looks like it. Let's not forget, if Doug used SAPD for the stop and found the money, they'd have to give the PD a cut. They used DPS to make the stop near Lytle. DPS didn't care what they were looking for and just drove off after the traffic stop was made."

Val and Brent just stared at Ricky. Finally, Val said, "You know, I don't give a shit about being in on the stop. Or having our picture taken with the money. But our group really could have used a cut of that money to help with operations. The city only gives us a little money to do a few small buys. It would have been nice to have enough money to do investigations like a big city department. After all, we are responsible for putting the DEA on to that trailer." Ricky replied, "I agree with you one hundred percent, Val. You identified the trailer from the wire, and Brent and the others got out on the road and found it. Then they arranged for the PD patrol unit to get it stopped. Your unit should have been in on a cut of the money. I wish I had more to give you, but all I have is the tail number of a Learjet." Brent said, "What the hell does the tail number of some damned Learjet do for us?" Ricky said, "I don't know, maybe nothing. But I heard Doug on the phone the other day. Someone was telling him about a Learjet owned by the cartel. They were speculating the Hernandez Cartel is using it to cross loads of dope. And then again, maybe they're using it to get their money back to Mexico. It does make some sense. Unless something unusual happens, the jet is not subject to regular customs inspections. Private planes land on a strip near the private hangers." Brent asked, "Are you telling me private planes flying into the US from Mexico without being subject to inspection." Ricky explained, "That's exactly what I'm telling you. Unless customs decide to spot check a plane, or there is some reason to believe they are hauling contraband, they come and go without being checked. This jet is one of the assets of a tour company owned by the cartel. If you can find that Learjet before Doug does, you can sure cause him to have a bad day."

Brent said, "The captain told us not to step on one of Doug's cases again. In fact, he gave us a direct order. Messing with that jet, if were able to find it, could be a problem for us. Doug has the Chief's ear, and both are assholes." Ricky stated, "Oh, I have confidence in you two. After all, it was quite a coincidence how the Eddie Coronado case fell into your lap. Hell, you didn't know that was going to be related to the Hernandez case. Maybe you could figure out how to handle another one the same way.

You might have a very hot tip on an incoming flight. Those flights come and go sometimes very quickly. Occasionally they will refuel, pick up a passenger, and be back in the air in a few minutes. If things were happening that quickly, you wouldn't have time to discuss it with anyone. If you knock off a big load of dope or money, I don't think anyone in the department would have a problem with you just doing your job. I would love to see y'all really stick it to Doug."

Val said, "I like the sound of it, but what if we jumped the plane and don't find anything? Doug will scream to high heaven we screwed up another one of his cases. He'll swear up and down he was just about to do something with that jet." Ricky said, "I didn't say it was going to be easy or without risk. I just thought if anybody had the balls to do it, it would be you two."

Brent still being a little apprehensive about anything that came from the DEA said, "I appreciate you giving this to us Ricky, but we're going to have to give this some thought. If we mess with this jet and don't score, it could be bad. I don't know what they would do. I guess we could get fired over it. Besides, what the hell are we going to do, sit out at the private plane terminal day and night looking for that tail number?" Ricky said, "I don't know, Brent. I know a tail number isn't much, but it's all I got. I know the DEA has called customs at the airport asking them to be on the lookout for that tail number. I was hoping y'all might have somebody out there you can trust to keep it under their hat while they watched for it." It took Val and Brent about two seconds to have the same idea, they turned to look at each other. They were both wide-eyed and said at the same time, "René!"

The next day, Brent called his old friend he used to work with in the homicide. "Hey Rene, how the new job going?" Rene replied, "Hey Brent, it's good. How are you?" Brent explained, "Look René, Val and I were talking about it yesterday and we want to buy you lunch tomorrow. I haven't seen you in a long time. We'd both like to hear about things at the airport. How about it, can we pick you up tomorrow and take you to lunch?"

Rene was curious but cautious, "Yeah, okay, but what made you think about me now. I haven't talked to you since before I retired." Brent said, "Well, Val and I both feel bad about missing your retirement party. We thought we could make up for it, in a small way by taking you to lunch. We'll pick you up at the airport tomorrow at noon." Rene replied, "Okay, I'm looking forward to it."

Val and Brent picked up Rene from the airport the next day and drove him to one of the most expensive steakhouses in town. As Brent drove into the parking lot of the restaurant, Rene was surprised. He said, "Man, you guys really are trying to make it up to me. I can't believe you brought me here. I've never been here before. I know some guys that have, and they tell me it's the best steak in town. When you said you wanted to make up for missing my retirement party, you decided to do it right."

Val, Brent and Rene were seated at a linen topped roundtable. After they were in their seats, Rene started looking around. He was impressed by the restaurant and flattered that Brent and Val would take him there. He thought I'm surprised at these two guys, I figured they would take me out for a hamburger, but look where we are, I may eat the best steak I've ever had. Brent and Val smiled as they looked at Rene. Then they saw Rene's smile fade. As Rene's face went from happy to sad, he said, "Wait a minute, what the hell is going on here? What are you going to do, stick me with the bill? I think I got this figured out. After we eat, your both going to get up and say you're going to the bathroom. Then you're going to walk out and leave me here with a bill for three hundred dollars."

With a surprised look on his face, Brent said, "Rene, I'm shocked. We offer to take you to lunch at one of the best places in town, and you accuse us of sticking you with the bill. I can't believe you would say anything like that." Rene said, "Okay, then, what do you want?" Brent with a wry smile said, "Well, Val and I do have a little favor to ask."

Rene thought he had this figured out and said, "Here we go, I knew it. Brent, I can't get you a job. I'm only the assistant chief. You'd have to talk to the chief about that." Brent said, "Rene, I don't want a job. I still have three years before I retire. All were asking you to do is keep an eye out for a private plane." Rene asked, "A private plane, what kind of private plane?" Brent explained, "It's a Learjet. We have the tail number and it will have a Mexican flag painted on the tail." Rene thought about for a few seconds and asked, "If you're looking for a Learjet from Mexico, why don't you just let customs watch for it?" Val stated, "We'd rather not get the fed's involved in it yet." Rene was now getting somewhat nervous with the topic of discussion and said, "Oh, so you want me to let you know when a Mexican Learjet comes in and you don't want customs involved. It sounds like your trying to get me fired. I haven't even had time to soak up some of this easy money. You're going to have to give me more than that, Brent." Brent replied, "Rene, you don't want to know everything. It's best for you to be able to say, that's the first I've heard about it. I would think all you need to know is, it's a favor to Harry." With bringing up his fallen friend, Rene asked, "Harry...this has something to do with Harry's murder?" Brent said, "Yes, the people who own the jet are responsible for his murder."

Rene scratched his head and it was easy to see he was thinking it over. Val said, "Rene, you don't have to worry about the fall out. If we get lucky and find the jet, we'll never let anyone know how we found it. You have our word on that." Brent could see Rene was still concerned and said, "Rene, if we could do it another way we would. Just keep an eye out for planes coming in to the private terminal. Hell, the odds are you'll never see it, but if you do, just give us a call. We'll take it from there. There may be a little dust up if we find it, but we'll never cause you any trouble. It's a shot in the dark Rene, but it's all we got." Rene took a deep breath then said, "Ok, if it'll help you make a case on Harry's killers, I'll do it. I'll watch for that tail number. But I can't be watching twenty-four hours a day. I'll do what I can." Val and

Brent leaned back in their chairs with big smiles on their faces and Brent said, "What did I tell you, Val. Didn't I tell you we could count on Rene?" Still with a concerned look on his face and a little apprehension in his voice Rene said, "If I spot that plane and it all works out, you two are going to have to bring me here once a month for the rest of your lives'." Val gladly replied, "You got it Rene. Now, why don't we enjoy these steaks?"

The following Monday morning, Jimmy and Mingo got back to work after their fishing trip. Val and Brent briefed them on the conversation they had with Rene. Mingo was excited about knocking off a load of Hernandez dope in a Learjet. Mingo said, "This is damned exciting, I've never made a traffic stop on a jet before. I've jacked up trucks, trailers, cars and motorcycles, but never a jet." A little more subdued, Brent said, "Well it's a long shot Rene will spot the jet. He's only there eight hours a day. He can't be watching the private terminal the whole time." Mingo had high hopes and said," Maybe, but there's still a chance." Jimmy was also subdued, not because of the long shot, he was worried about the consequences. Jimmy said, "I don't know about this. The captain told us not to mess with the DEA. I really want to hurt the Hernandez Cartel, but this could be the last thing we do as police officers. I could always get a job with my brother roofing, but I don't like swinging hammers anymore." Val said, "What is it you think we shouldn't do? Not do our job. Isn't the city paying us to make dope cases?" Jimmy said, "Sure, but the chief gave us a direct order not to get involved with the Hernandez case again." Brent said, "The way I see it is, sometimes you don't know who the dope belongs to until after you make the case." Jimmy said, "If it works out everything's fine. You'll be able to play it off. What if you jack up that plane and there's a bunch of tourists in it? The DEA's going to raise hell and the chief is going to fire you. At the very least, you'll get demoted. Are you sure you want to go back to making calls and handling accidents?" Brent sternly said, "I still feel responsible Harry and the patrolman dying after I took them out there. This is just a chance I must take. I don't think I could live with myself knowing I had a chance to put some of these guys in federal prison for the rest of their lives and didn't do it because I was scared of being demoted or losing my job." Stunned by Brent's, scared remark Jimmy said, "I didn't say I was scared, just a little worried, I guess. All I'm saying is I'm going to have to think about it, that's all." Brent said, "You don't have to go out there if Rene calls, Jimmy. That's up to you. But if we get a chance to see what that plane is hauling, I'm going. I know Val is in, what about you, Mingo?" Mingo said, "I don't give a damn about the chief, if it goes bad, I'll just retire. I've got my thirty years in the books. The old lady has been trying to get me to retire for years. I'm just not ready yet. What am I going to do if I retire, sit on the porch all day in a rocking chair and drink beer? I like drinking beer with y'all. I know how it goes with being a retiree. Two months after I'm gone, you won't even remember me. You'll be saying, Mingo who? No, I'll take my chances on this one." Val said, "I'm with Mingo on this one. I've got twenty-seven years. I can retire too. Brent, I guess you and Jimmy are the ones with the most to lose. You know Brent, Mingo and I can go out there and deal with that plane. Why don't you and Jimmy hang back. If it goes right, we'll give you a call. If it doesn't, you can say you didn't know anything about it." Brent said, "You can just forget all about that. As much as I want to make them pay for what they did to Harry, it's also a chance for a once in a lifetime case. No, if Rene calls, I'm going."

Chapter 15 Woops

It was twenty-seven days after Val and Brent briefed Mingo and Jimmy. They told them about Rene and the Learjet. After roll call, Sgt. Clower looked at Mingo and said, "Mingo, I want to see you in my office. I'd like to talk to you about your job. Well, I mean the job you're not doing." Val, Jimmy and Brent whistled and made cat calls as Mingo dropped his head before standing and walking to the sergeant's office. After entering the office, Sgt. Clower said, "Close the door, Mingo and have a seat." Mingo sat in front of the desk and Clower sat behind it. Clower said, "Mingo, what the hell is wrong with you. Are you sick or something? Has Cindy told you to stop drinking, or have you just lost your mind due to old age?"

"What do you mean, Donnie. I'm not having any trouble. What would make you think a thing like that?" Clower continued, "What do I mean? You haven't made a case in six months. I know you've got enough time to retire and everybody slacks off a little when they get to retirement age but come on! You gotta do something around here." Mingo said, "I know Donnie, but one of my CI's has been sick and the other one's in jail. I told that knucklehead to stop stealing, but you know how they are. You tell 'em and you tell 'em, but they don't listen. Sometimes I think I'm working for them, not the other way around." Clower replied, "Yeah, I know how they are, and I know how you are. Your just plain lazy. If you go any longer without making a case, what are the other guys going to think? If I give them a hard time about low productivity, they're going to say, Mingo doesn't do anything, why should I?" Mingo was pleading, "Donnie, it's tough to get anything done when I don't have a decent CI. I've asked some of the daylight guys if they can throw me a bone, but they're not helping me out. I can't go make a buy, I've never done that before. Come on,

Donnie, were old friends. Give a buddy a break. I'm working on something, I'm just about to hit a house. I already started typing the warrant. I was thinking about running it today."

Sgt Clower concluded, "That's a good idea. I'm taking heat from the brass. They looked at our stats and saw you're not doing anything. You should give me a break! It looks like I'm not doing a good job supervising. If you're working on a warrant, you better run it soon."

As he was hurrying out of the office Mingo said, 'Ok Donnie, I'll run it today"

During Mingo's counseling, Brent looked at Jimmy and said, "Hey Jimmy, there was so much going on when you got back, I forgot to ask you about the fishing trip. Did you do any good?" Jimmy replied, "We did okay. We caught a few but not like we've done before. You never have been to the land cut, have you Brent?" "No, I haven't" replied Brent. Jimmy asked, "Why don't you go with us? I know you like to fish. What's the deal, don't you like our company, or what?" Brent explained, "I just don't like the sound of roughing it like y'all do. I mean, spending a week in a broken-down old cabin with no power or running water doesn't sound like a good time to me. Not to mention, you have to leave here at 2 a.m. before the wind starts blowing on the bay. You get there after a four-hour drive, just to take an hour boat ride across the bay. It sounds like a lot of trouble." Jimmy said, "Yeah, but that adds to the adventure. The cabins ok, it has some holes in the walls, but that lets the wind come through. It has running water. There's a barrel on top of the cabin that catches rain water. The waters cold but you can still get a shower. That is, maybe once during the trip." Brent asked, "One shower in a week? Let me ask you this. How does Mingo and the rest of your fishing buddies smell after three days in the sun? And how do you get any sleep with all the snoring that goes on in there? I've heard Mingo snore. I'd rather sleep next to railroad tracks than hear that all night." Jimmy replied, "It's not bad, you can't hear Mingo snore over the noises the lighthouse makes. There's electricity too. There's a generator we use to watch tv and run a fan and the lights." Brent responded, "Well Jimmy if that suits you, that's great. I always choose to fish in Rockport. It only takes me about an hour and a half to get there. Besides, I like air conditioning, running water, satellite TV, you know, little things like that." Jimmy pressed, "Oh, what a puss! As far as Mingo's snoring goes, you don't hear it if you get drunk enough!" Brent said, "If I drank enough to block out Mingo's snoring, I'd be sick for the rest of the trip. I don't want to spend four hours driving. I we left at the same time to go fishing I'd have lines in the water and you'd still be two and a half hours from the boat ramp. Why would I drive that far when I can catch fish in less than half the time?" Jimmy replied, "Brent, it's not about the drive or the fishing. It's about the comradery and experience." Brent was getting agitated, "The experience? You mean the experience of being cooped up in a rickety old cabin with a bunch of stinky old men." Brent glanced over to where a janitors' cleaning cart was left outside the bathroom door. "Well, Jimmy, I can save you some time. If it's not about fishing, why don't you fish in that mop bucket over there. It'll be cheaper, and you'd still be around your buddies for the comradery. The hole group will even smell better." Brent and Jimmy stared at each other for a few seconds and Jimmy said, "You're an idiot."

Mingo walked out of the sergeant's office and said, "Well, I guess I can't put off making a case anymore. I hate to write reports. Donnie says I haven't made a case in three months." Brent said, "Three months, I don't remember you making a case since I stopped riding with you. I got news for you Mingo, I'm not getting in your car to go out and choke a street dealer." Mingo sat at his desk and typed for about thirty seconds. He stood up and said, "I'm going to go get a paper signed." Brent laughed and said, "Oh shit, Mingo. You're going to run a warrant? Who are we going to hit?" Mingo replied, "We'll go hit Andy Gonzalez." Val moaned rolled his eyes and said, "Andy Gonzalez, we never find anything over there. It's a waste of time." Mingo replied, "Yeah maybe, but I got to do something to get the sergeant off my back." Jimmy said, "Mingo, Val's right, we never find anything there. If you're not there thirty minutes after he gets a load, he'll have it stashed. We know when he had that house built, he had hiding places custom made in the walls and floors. You got any information on him?"

Mingo said, "Yeah, I have lots of information on him. He's a doper. That's all the information I need. I've had that information for twenty-five years. I know he's a dealer, and he knows he's a dealer. Besides, Andy won't mind getting hit. He expects to get hit once in a while. He knows it's the cost of doing business." Val said, "That's true, I've never met a more gracious trafficker. He's always been very pleasant when we show up with a warrant." Mingo laughed and said, "His dad was the same way. We'd show up and he would invite us in. His wife would ask us if we wanted a glass of iced tea while we searched." Brent said, "I've always thought it was funny how his house looks on that street. All the houses around his are worth about thirty thousand and his is worth half a million. I wonder why he doesn't just move to a fancier neighborhood?" Mingo replied, "It's because everyone on that block is on his payroll. If a strange car rolls down the street, he gets ten calls from the neighbors." Jimmy said, "If I lived there, I'd be on the payroll too. It's the safest street in town. Every burglar knows if' they steal there, they won't be alive much longer. How 'bout that, a crime free street on the westside. The city should hire Andy as a crime prevention expert."

Mingo went to get the warrant signed and four detectives got into two cars to drive to Andy's house. They parked in front of the house and walked to the door. Mingo said, "There's no sense in getting in a big hurry. Andy's had five calls by now letting him know we're here." Mingo rang the doorbell and Andy opened the door. Andy said, "Hello, Mingo, where you been? I haven't seen you in a while." Andy looked at the others and said, "Hello Jimmy, Val and shook their hands." He then looked at Brent and said, "I don't believe we've met, I'm Andy." Brent shook Andy's hand and said, "I'm Brent, I hope we're not intruding." Andy said, "Not at all, I'm glad you came by. Mingo and Val used to come by here occasionally to visit my dad. Didn't you Mingo?" Mingo said, "Andy, we're going to search for a little while. Can we come in?" Andy replied, "Sure, sure. Honey, Mingo and Val are here!"

Mingo, Val, Jimmy and Brent walked in to see Andy had house guests. Mingo said, "I didn't know you were entertaining, Andy. This shouldn't take long. Would you and your wife please have a seat in the living room with your two guests?"

Val and Brent went into the master bedroom to begin their search. Mingo went outside to check the shed. Jimmy started looking around in the utility room. Val and Brent were searching the bedroom halfheartedly. Val found a VCR tape on a shelf in the closet labeled "Personal". Val picked it up and said, "Uh oh, I wonder what's on here, Brent?" Val put it into the VCR and turned on the TV. Val hit play on the tape player, but there wasn't a picture on the TV, just a black screen. The TV came on after Brent shook some wires and flipped a switch behind the TV. Sure, enough the movie started playing and it was a tape of Andy and his young wife involved in a romantic encounter. Brent made a rude remark and said, "Boom chica, bow wow." They made lewd comments as they watched.

After searching the shed, Mingo walked back into the living room. He saw Andy's guests and wife sitting on the couch with their heads held down in their hands. Mingo heard odd noises and looked at the living room TV. Mingo ran into the master bedroom and discovered how the video was started. Mingo said, "Hey you two idiots, that tape is playing on the TV!" Val said, "So what, we'll put it back in a minute." Mingo screamed, "It's playing on the living room TV, moron!"

When Brent moved switches behind the TV in the bedroom, he fed the image into the living room. Brent said, "Oh shit", and frantically tried to turn it off. He didn't even know how he got it started and didn't know how to stop it. They finally got the video stopped and figured they'd been there long enough. The only thing they'd done was screw up. All four ended the so called, "search". One by one, they walked to the door with Mingo bringing up the rear. Just before Mingo walked out, Andy said, "Hey Mingo, call next time before you come. I'll have dinner waiting."

Chapter 16 The Bust at the Airport

Mingo, Val, Jimmy and Brent left Andy's house after running Mingo's, "search warrant". They managed to waste their time, and Andy's. They were also able to mortify Andy's wife, and his two houseguests with the video that was screened in his living room. They didn't find any dope, but all things being equal, Mingo did have one search warrant to put on his monthly activity sheet. It certainly wasn't the French connection, but at least he had something to show Sgt. Clower.

After regrouping at the office, they drove to a nearby pool hall. They'd just started their third game. Brent was about to break the rack. He was glad to start the third game because he and Val already beat Jimmy and Mingo out of fifty dollars in the first two games. Just as Brent was about to shoot his phone rang. Brent answered, "Hello". "Brent, its Rene. You guys better get here quick. Your plane is about fifteen minutes from being handed over to the ground crew." Stunned by what Rene had to say Brent asked, "Are you sure, Rene? I mean, you've seen it?" Rene was excited and stated, "Yes I'm sure. Do you think I would make a joke out of something like this? The tail number matches the one you gave me, and it has a big Mexican flag painted on the tail. You better get your ass over here quick. This opportunity may not last very long." Brent looked at the others with wide eyes and with an excited voice he said, "The Jets on the ground!"

Mingo was giving Jimmy grief about the gambling. He was in the middle of a lecture about how Jimmy was no better pool player than Harry. Mingo said, "Boy, sometimes I think I've got no luck at all and you are just another example, Jimmy. Harry's gone and I feel terrible about that, but I thought at least I might find a better pool playing partner. And I got news for you Jimmy, you ain't it." Jimmy said, "Oh give me a break, Mingo. I don't even like pool. I told you I didn't want to play. I'm not even betting. You know Mingo, when one guy doesn't want to bet on a pool game and he's your partner, you shouldn't bet either. You call yourself a high-class detective, but the FBI calls that a clue."

Val was on his phone and didn't hear what Brent said either. Brent noticed no one heard what he said and yelled, "Did you hear me you bunch of morons!" Now that got their attention. Mingo yelled back at Brent, "No I didn't hear you. What did you say?" Brent replied, "I said, Rene just called. The Learjet we told him about is on the ground. We may only have about fifteen minutes to get to the airport and see what's on that plane!"

All four hurried out of the pool hall and into the parking lot. They drove from the office to the pool hall in one car. Val unlocked the green T Bird and unlocked the other doors. Brent opened the passenger side door and jumped in while Mingo jumped in the driver side back seat. Jimmy opened the passenger side rear door, but didn't get in. Jimmy hesitated and stood in the parking lot looking into the car. Brent looked back at Jimmy and said, "What the hell are you doing, get in!" Jimmy answers, "I don't know Brent, I think it's a little risky." Aggravated, Brent responded, "Yeah it's a little risky. We've already talked about that. Now get in!" Even after Brent yelling at Jimmy to get in, Jimmy stood still. Brent was fuming, and in a low deep angry tone Brent told Jimmy, "Jimmy, we don't have time for this. Now get your ass in the car or get the hell out of the way." After staring at Jimmy for three seconds and seeing Jimmy was still standing in the parking lot, Brent looked at Val and screamed, "Let's go!" Val took one quick look back at Jimmy. Jimmy was still frozen in place. Val turned his face forward looking through the windshield, then hit the gas. Jimmy didn't close the door, but as Val's T Bird spun its back tires, the door closed by itself. It took eleven minutes for Val to get his T Bird from the pool hall to the private terminal of the San Antonio Airport. He drove up to the gate and stopped at the guard shack. Val rolled down his window and spoke to the security guard. As Val displayed his police ID, Val said, "We're with the PD narcotics office. We'd like to check out a private plane that just arrived. Can you help us with that?" The guard answered, "Yeah, I guess so. Wait here while I call my supervisor." Val frantically said, "I don't mean to rush you, but we don't have much time. The plane is on the ground and we can't miss who gets out of it." "Okay, my sergeants in that terminal. Why don't you go in there and I'll have him meet you."

Val sped his car to the front of the terminal. A sergeant with airport security was waiting at the front of the building. Val, Brent and Mingo jumped out the car. The security sergeant asked, "What's going on? The guard at the gate told me you needed to meet a private plane." Brent said, "I just got word about a private plane landing. We suspect it may be loaded with cocaine. The flight originated in Mexico." That caused the security sergeant to raise her eyebrows and without any more questions or comments, the sergeant walked the guys out the back of the terminal and onto the taxiway. Five different private planes were lined up there waiting for the ground crew to take over.

Brent pulled a small notepad out of his shirt pocket looking for the tail number he got from Ricky. He flipped through a few pages when Val said, "I see it." There was only one aircraft in the lineup that displayed a Mexican flag on the tail them. Val raised his right hand, pointed toward the lineup and said, "That has to be the one." The airport sergeant looked at the three detectives and asked, "What do you want to do? How can I help?" Brent said, "We need to search it and identify the pilots."

The airport sergeant walked to one of the grounds crewmen and said, "Flag that one for inspection." As he pointed toward the plane that Val picked out. Val, Mingo and Brent stood at the side of the taxiway and watched as the jet slowly made its way to the terminal. The jet powered down. One of the members of the grounds crew was standing on the left side of the plane when it stopped. The plane lowered the exit ladder. Shortly after, two men, the pilot and copilot walked down the ladder. Val, Mingo, Brent and the security sergeant walked up to the two men just as they stepped on the ground. Val began the conversation, he asked the two men, "Do you speak English?" The man standing to Brent's right said, "Yes, I do, I'm the pilot." Val said, "Good, where did your flight originate?" The pilot answered, "Guadalajara." Val asked the pilot, "Who owns this aircraft?" The pilot hesitated for a moment and then answered, "It's owned by a tourist company in Mexico. I'm a pilot working for the company." Val then asked, "Who owns the tourist company?" The pilot replied, "Oh, I don't know about that. I mean, I've never even met the people at the business. I just get phone calls from their representative letting me know when they want a flight to go out." Val continued his questioning, "Why don't you know who owns the company, you get a check don't you?" The pilot replied, "Yes, I get a check, but I'm contracted for the flights. I fly out and fly back, and a few days later I get a check in the mail. I just don't know anything about the owner of the business." Val then asked, "Is there anyone else in the plane? If you're not bringing anything in and there's no one on board, why did you fly here? The pilot responded, "We were sent here to pick up some business files, then fly back." Val had a surprised look on his face when he asked the pilot, "Are you telling me you flew in to pick up paperwork? Who is giving you the paperwork?" The pilot said, "I don't know, someone is supposed to bring us the paperwork tonight at the hotel. Then we'll fly back tomorrow." Val continued, "You have no idea who's supposed to bring you the files?" The pilot was now getting agitated with the line of questioning and responded, "No, I don't. I guess it's supposed to be someone from the travel agency." Val was now on a roll and asked, "Why would someone ask you to fly from

Guadalajara to San Antonio to pick up files? Wouldn't it be a lot cheaper to send them UPS?"

Now the pilot of the plane was getting aggravated by the questions from Val, he said," Hey look, its none of my business. I am just told……. I mean, we're just told what to do and we do it." Val questioned, "Is there anything in the plane right now? Are there any boxes, luggage or any other sort of container in there?" The pilot explained, "No there's nothing. Me and the copilot were the only thing in the plane when it landed." Brent asked the airport police sergeant, "Would it be all right for us to take a look around in the plane?" The sergeant said, "Sure, all incoming planes are subject to inspection. But I think it would be best if customs were here for the search." Val said, "Ok, I'd like to do it right away. Can you get them out here for us?" The sergeant replied, "Yeah, there are customs agents assigned here. They can be out here in a few minutes." The sergeant made the call to the customs desk. One of the two agents answered and told him he would be right there. The agent who answered the phone told the other, "I'm going to help some narcotics guys search a plane. The other agent said, "Ok, I wonder if those guys are with Doug Garlands group?"

The first asked, "Who's Doug Garland?" The second agent explained, "He's a friend of mine. When I was going through the customs academy, he was becoming a DEA agent. He's a group supervisor now." While the first customs agent was making his way to the private plane terminal, the second agent called Doug and asked, "Hey Doug, is this your crew out here with the plane? I thought you would be with them.

I just wanted to say hello when you got here." Doug said, "I don't have any guys at the airport." The agent explained, "Well, there's some guys out here that say they're with narcotics. They want to search a Learjet." Doug yelled, "Wait a minute! Can you see the tail number from where you are?" The customs agent picked up a pair of binoculars and looked toward the plane. He could see the red tail number and repeated it to Doug. Doug then looked down at his desk calendar where he wrote the information he received about the Hernandez plane. The number matched. Doug said, "Try to hold what you got!" After he slammed down the phone, he yelled so loud the whole office thought he might be having a stroke. "Those bastards have jumped our case again!"

As Doug raced to his car, he called Jamie Aleman, the Special Agent in Charge of the San Antonio DEA office. "Jamie, those local yokels have stepped on our Hernandez Cartel case again. Didn't you call the police chief?" Jamie replied, "Yeah, I talked to the chief. He assured me he would make sure his guys didn't get involved with your case again. Why, what's going on?" Doug instructed, "Meet me at the private plane terminal at the airport. They're messing with the plane we've been looking for. They may have screwed up our whole case!"

On the way to the airport, SAC Aleman called the San Antonio Police Chief. Aleman said, "Chief, it's Jamie. Your boys have stepped on our case again and I'm pretty pissed off about it. I was hoping you could take care of this. Didn't you talk to their captain?" The police chief always wanting to stay in the good graces of the Feds said, "I'm sorry Jamie, what have they done now?" Jamie explained, "They are at the private terminal of the airport. I don't have all the details yet, but it's not good. Why don't you meet me there? We need to put a stop to this once and for all." The chief replied, "Don't you worry about it, Jamie, I'll have all of them relieved of duty as soon as I get there. They are done doing police work." As the chief got into the back seat of his black suburban, looking more like a head of state rather than a public servant, he had his personal driver speed toward the airport. The chief got on his phone and called Capt. Smith. "Terry, I thought I told you to keep those assholes away from the DEA case. Were you listening to me?" Acting as if he was confused, Capt. Terry Smith asked the chief, "Which assholes are you talking about? I've got a lot of them. Can you be a little more specific?" The chief was in no mood to be humored with, "Don't be a smart ass with me, Terry. You know which assholes I'm talking about. Those idiot narcs that keep screwing with that DEA case. You better get over to the private terminal at the airport right now. You and those idiots have a lot explaining to do." Smith replied, "Yeah, okay, I'm on the way." Captain Smith hung up the phone and mumbled, "Son of a bitch. These guys are killing me."

Val, Brent and Mingo were about to get their first look at the inside of the plane. Now tensions were running very high. They knew their jobs were probably on the line. Standing outside the door of the Learjet, Val took a deep breath, looked at Brent and said, "I sure hope there's a pile of kilos in this plane. Or at least a bunch of boxes or dead bodies or something." Brent responded meekly, "Yeah, me too." Brent walked up the small latter extended from the plane and entered the aircraft. Val followed while Mingo waited outside. Bending over at the waist, Brent and Val made their way through the small aircraft. They walked from the front to the back, looking side to side as they went. They didn't find anything, not even a scrap of paper. It was completely empty. No cocaine, no money, nothing. Val and Brent turned to each other inside the plane. They stood quietly for a moment. Val walked down the staircase followed by Brent and stood on the ground in front of Mingo. Mingo new by looking at them it was probably bad news. Then Mingo asked, "Well?" Brent felt sick to his stomach and couldn't speak. Val looked at Mingo said, "No." Trying to raise their hopes, Mingo said, "Maybe it's hidden." Mingo made his way through the plane. He searched high and low for something that would make their efforts worthwhile, knowing there was a lot on the line for all of them.

Val and Brent stood next to the plane silently with their heads hanging down. Val looked at Brent and said, "Let's get out of here. We haven't given our names to anyone, maybe they'll never figure it out." Just as Val and Brent were considering loading up and driving away, cars started filing into the gate. First was Doug Garland, then his supervisor special agent in charge, Jamie Aleman. They were followed by the San Antonio police chief, and then Capt. Smith. Doug was the first one out of his car and immediately started screaming at Val and Brent, "I don't know how you did this, but I'm going to find out! I hope you're happy about what you've done! You've probably killed our whole case!"

Standing behind Garland was Jamie and the police chief. The chief was trying to smooth things over with Aleman saying, "Don't you worry Jamie, I'm going to the fire these guys for disobeying a direct order. If the lawyers with the Police Officers Association can stop the firing order, they'll be writing parking tickets for the rest of their careers!"

Mingo was on the plane and couldn't see what was happening outside. He didn't see the head of the department and the head of the DEA regional office. Looking at Val, Mingo said, "If it's in here, I can't find it." After seeing the chief, Jamie Aleman, Doug Garland and Capt. Smith, Mingo said, "I guess running away is out of the question." The chief turned to Capt. Smith and said, "Terry you talk to these idiots? They make me sick." The chief was always known for his affection for the rank and file members of the police force.

Capt. Smith walked up to Val, Mingo and Brent as the chief, Aleman and Garland walked to the terminal. Capt. Smith asked, "Well, did you at least find something?" Val answered, "No." Capt. Smith dropped his head and said, "Boy, we are all going to take some heat over this. How much heat, I don't know? Val, you and Mingo can retire but Brent, they're going to fire you. I hope all that happens to me is a demotion. Maybe I can be a detective again." Brent said, "It's my fault, this was my idea." The captain sighed and said, "We'll have plenty of time to talk about whose fault it is." As he looked at the pilot and copilot Capt. Smith asked, "What are you going to do with these two guys?" Brent said, "Not that it will make any difference to me, but I guess we can take them in to the customs office and get them printed. If somebody comes across them in the future, at least there will be a record of them."

Val, Mingo, Brent and the captain walked the pilot and copilot into the terminal. They took them into the customs office where Val asked the customs agent to print them and get them into the AFIS computer system. The customs agent began printing the pilot first using the AFIS terminal. As the pilot was being printed, the chief and Jamie Aleman walked into the print office. The chief looked at Capt. Smith and said, "Terry I just want you to know I'm going to transfer you tomorrow. I don't think I can fire you, but you will surely be demoted. As far as the Three Stooges here, you can consider that there are there indefinite suspensions beginning today."

The chief belittled Capt. Smith and the group for the benefit of Jamie. It always seemed the chief was searching for a job at whatever higher level he could suck up to. The customs agent was finished printing the pilot and started scanning the prints of the copilot. He scanned the last of the copilot's fingers and entered the prints into the system. Immediately a response came back. The customs agent yelled, "Holly shit!" as he stared at the copilot and asked the assembled group, "Do you know who this guy is?" The three detectives, the chief, Aleman and the captain looked at the agent in amazement. The agent then exclaimed, "It's Daniel Raymundo Hernandez!"

The chief was aware of all the excitement but didn't understand, which was not unusual. Then he asked the agent, "Who?"

All were stunned by the revelation. Aleman asked the customs agent, "Are you sure?" The agent said, "Come here and look at this." As Aleman looked at the screen he saw,

"INTERNATIONAL FUGITIVE……USE

EXTREME CAUTION……KNOWN FOR VIOLENCE…."

Brent reached into his back pocket, grabbed a pair of handcuffs and slapped them onto the wrists of Daniel Raymundo Hernandez. Still stunned by all that happened, the chief looked at Jamie and asked, "What's going on here? Is this good?" Jamie looked at the chief still with a stunned look on his face and said, "They just caught one of the world's most wanted criminals!" Hearing this from outside the door, Doug rushed in and said, "I'm taking custody of him! I have some guys on the way to handle, our, prisoner!" Doug walked Hernandez out of the customs office and then out of the terminal toward his car. The chief looked at SAC Aleman and asked, "What do you make of all of this, Jamie?" Jamie walked out of the print office and toward the exit of the terminal with the chief in tow. Capt. Smith, Mingo, Val and Brent could hear Aleman telling the chief, "Chief, I think this is going to go to the press as a great example for the rest of the country to see. It shows when a local police department and the DEA work together, great things can be accomplished." They could also hear the chief say, "That's exactly what I was thinking, Jamie. I always feel that having the two groups working together will achieve great things."

After all the critics were gone, Capt. Smith looked at Val, Mingo and Brent and said, "I have never in my life seen three guys that could fall backwards in a pile of crap and come out smelling like a rose like you three just did."

The case resulted in 7 cartel members being sentenced to life in federal prison. Houses in one of San Antonio's most expensive subdivisions and several exclusive restaurants were awarded as the proceeds of money laundering. Truck tractors, trailers, passenger cars and trucks involved in narcotics trafficking were seized. Approximately 12 million dollars in cash, 300 kilos of cocaine, 500,000 tabs of Ecstasy were recovered. The total dollar amount estimated on the of property, cash and narcotics seizures was more than 100 million dollars. The 17 passenger Learjet found at the airport was awarded to the DEA.

Made in the USA
Las Vegas, NV
18 January 2022